Moving Right Along

Other Doubleday Science Experiment Books that you will enjoy

Moving Right Along

A BOOK OF SCIENCE EXPERIMENTS AND PUZZLERS ABOUT MOTION

By Robert Gardner and David Webster

Illustrated with photographs
and with line drawings by Tang-Fung Cho

DOUBLEDAY & COMPANY, INC.
GARDEN CITY, NEW YORK

Library of Congress Cataloging in Publication Data

Gardner, Robert, 1929–
    Moving right along.

    SUMMARY: Discusses various aspects of the science
of motion and includes suggestions for related
experiments.
    1. Motion—Juvenile literature. [1. Motion]
I. Webster, David, 1930– joint author. II. Cho,
Tang Fung. III. Title.
QC127.4.G37   531′.11′028
ISBN 0-385-11642-x Trade
      0-385-11643-8 Prebound
Library of Congress Catalog Card Number 77–15149

Contents

Preface

Can you imagine a world where nothing is moving—a motionless, soundless, lifeless planet frozen in space? It would be a strange place indeed! You could not hear the wind, rustling leaves, or traffic horns. There would be total silence. The sun, moon, and stars would appear to hang forever motionless in space. One side of the earth would be in daylight all the time; the other side would always be dark. Clouds would not move, rain would not fall, and brooks and rivers would not flow. All life would end, for without motion, nothing could live.

The real world is far more interesting because it is filled with moving things. You are a vibrant part of this motion-filled world. In fact, you, or parts of you, are in constant motion. When you run, ride your bike, or even read a book, it is obvious that you are moving. But even when you lie perfectly still or sleep, your chest rises and falls as you breathe and your pulse throbs softly.

If you could look inside your body, you would find your heart pumping about once each second, sending blood rushing into arteries that swell with each beat and then contract, forcing the blood outward to all parts of your body. You would see food being churned, turned, and mixed with juices flowing into your intestines. You would find air moving into and out of the many tiny sacs that form your lungs.

Just as you are filled with motion from within, you are surrounded by motion on the outside. You can see birds and airplanes moving gracefully through the air above the earth. On windy days, the invisible air moves tree branches and scatters loose papers in the street. Vehicles of all sizes and shapes whiz along highways in an endless procession. People and other animals are moving almost constantly. Even when you watch TV, you blink your eyes and wiggle around in your chair. See how uncomfortable it is to stay perfectly still for even a few minutes?

There are still more moving things that you do not usually notice. Many are moving too slowly for you to see. It takes the ocean tide about six hours to change from low to high. The hour hand of a clock goes around once in twelve hours. Your fingernails grow only about one-quarter inch each month. You can detect the movement of such slow things by observing them over a long time. Look at the ocean shoreline every few hours or your nails every few days. The slower something moves, the longer you must wait before being aware that it has changed position.

Many fast-moving things are so far away that they appear to move slowly. Clouds driven by a strong wind often seem to be nearly motionless. An airplane traveling at 600 miles an hour appears to be moving with stately slowness when high in the sky. The earth travels through space at even greater speeds, and yet you are unaware of its motion.

Other movements occur rapidly and close by, but are unnoticed because they cannot be seen. Water seeps slowly through the ground or flows quickly inside of pipes and sewer lines. Earthworms, ants, and other burrowing animals leave evidence of their motion with soil tunnels and miniature dirt piles. Invisible radio and sound waves move continually through the air around you. Motion is everywhere.

MOVING RIGHT ALONG is a book to help you learn more about the science of motion. You will find out what speed records have been set by animals, cars, and airplanes. There are experiments you can do to measure your own speed when running or riding a bicycle. More experiments can be done with a tiny air car, balloon rockets, pendulums, spinning eggs, water pistols, bicycles, and skateboards. At the end of the book there are a number of motion puzzles for you to solve.

Be sure to try the activities that interest you. Motion science is much more fun when you do the experiments to help explain what you read.

I

Speed Records

Men have always tried to move rapidly. Early cavemen probably engaged in foot races to test their running ability. Primitive man, though, ran mostly because he had to. Sometimes he pursued animals, trying to catch them for food. Other times he ran away even faster from bigger animals which wanted to eat *him*.

Organized races were first held in the Olympic Games in ancient Greece. The marathon run of 26 miles (42 kilometers) was a feature event. As man devised other means of travel, such as skis and iceboats, he was able to surpass his fastest running speed. With the development of engines to propel cars and airplanes, record speeds in the past one hundred years have increased greatly.

Speed records are kept for a great many forms of locomotion. Some men have spent their entire lives and much money attempting to break records set by speedboats, racing cars, and airplanes. Sometimes they succeed; other times they meet only failure and even death.

Vehicles can be conveniently classified into three main groups according to where they travel—through the water, on land, or in the air. A vehicle's maximum speed is determined only in part by the power of its motor. Equally important is how much resistance to motion the machine encounters because of friction. Since water has much greater resistance than air, speed records in water are considerably slower than land and air records.

Boat speed records

The bow of an outboard motorboat is pointed to reduce water friction. Speedboats such as hydroplanes are more saucer-shaped, since at high speeds they skim across the sur-

A Coast Guard hydrofoil. *U. S. Coast Guard Photo*

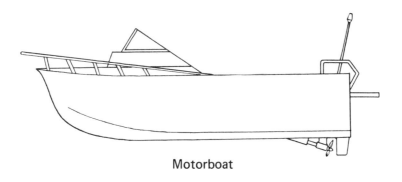

Motorboat

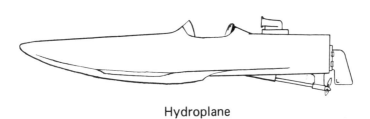

Hydroplane

Hull shapes of a hydroplane and a motorboat.

face of the water. Some boats, called *hydrofoils,* actually rise out of the water and slip along on ski-like fins. Friction is thus greatly reduced since none of the hull drags through the water.

The Coast Guard hydrofoil pictured can travel 50 miles per hour. When cruising on its hull, the 68-ton craft is powered by twin 200-horsepower diesel engines. A separate, 3,150-horsepower gas turbine propels the boat when it is foil-borne. Its crew consists of one officer and twelve enlisted men.

Table A shows the average top speed of outboard motorboats with motors of different horsepowers. Notice that doubling a motor's horsepower does not even nearly double the boat's speed. Of course, a boat's speed also depends upon its size and the weight of the people riding in it. Rough water, a strong tide, or a headwind can slow down a boat.

TABLE A: *Speed of boats with different-powered outboard motors.*

Power (hp) of motors	Average top speed (mph)
5	15
10	18
20	20
40	25
65	35
100	40
175	50

A boat towing a waterskier usually travels between 20 and 30 mph. If you have ever waterskied, you know you feel as if you are going a lot faster. Even riding in an open boat going only 15 mph feels much faster than the same speed in an automobile. This is partly because you are so close to the water and also because you feel a lot more "wind."

The world's fastest waterskier managed to hang on behind a big motorboat going 126 mph (203 kilometers per hour [kph]).

Table B shows the highest speeds attained by various types of boats and ships. Large ocean liners and navy destroyers are driven by gigantic steam turbines.

TABLE B: *Boat speed records.*

Type of boat	Record speed (mph)
Eight-man sculling boat	13
Yacht	32
Large ocean liner	40
Destroyer	51
Nuclear submarine (underwater)	52
Large hydrofoil	70
Speedboat (propeller-driven)	200
Speedboat (turbojet-driven)	328

The fastest speed ever attained over water was accomplished by Donald Campbell of Great Britain. Campbell inherited his interest in speed from his father, Sir Malcolm Campbell, who died in 1948 holding the water speed record of 141 mph. Another speedster, Stanley Sayres of Seattle, set a new mark of 178.497 mph in 1952. Donald returned the record to the Campbell family in 1955 when he drove his speedboat to a championship mark of 202.32 mph. In 1967 Donald Campbell attempted to break his own record on a lake in England in another boat powered by a turbojet engine. During his last run the 2¼ -ton craft reached the speed of 328 mph (528 kph). Suddenly, the boat broke into pieces, killing Campbell and ending his chance for an official record. While his 328-mph speed was accurately timed, it does not qualify

These hydroplanes were competing in the Gold Cup Race which is held each August under the auspices of the American Power Boat Association. *Courtesy of the Goodyear Motor Sports Club*

for an official world record. Two runs of one mile each in opposite directions must be timed and averaged together. This is to eliminate any time advantage gained by a tail wind or the direction of water current.

Railroad speeds

The earliest speed records on land were not set by racing cars, but by railroad trains. This was because the steam engine was invented many years before lighter, gasoline-powered engines. Early steam engines were so big that an extremely heavy vehicle was needed to carry them. The solution was a ponderous locomotive having steel wheels to roll along a level track. Remember, one hundred years ago there were no paved roads or rubber tires.

To qualify for a world speed record, the locomotive must pull at least four coaches. By 1839 an English steam engine known as *Lucifer* traveled at the then unheard-of speed of 59 mph. Only a few years later, in 1843, an Irish train powered by compressed air went 85 mph. This record lasted for some forty-seven years, until a steam train sped along a track in France at 89 mph. The next rail record was set in 1903 by a German electric train, which reached a speed of 131 mph. The current railroad records are 126 mph for a steam engine and 206 mph for an electric train. A new French *aerotrain*, powered by jet airplane engines and riding on a cushion of air, hit 235 mph in 1967. It took 128 years for railroad train speeds to increase from 59 mph to 235 mph.

The highest speed ever attained on rails is 3,090 mph (4,972 kph) by a rocket-powered sled in 1958. This was an unmanned test vehicle shot along a 6-mile track in New Mexico. The experiment was done to learn the effects of the high speeds that would be encountered in the spaceflight program of the National Aeronautics and Space Administration (NASA).

In an earlier test, a sled carrying a man traveled 623 mph.

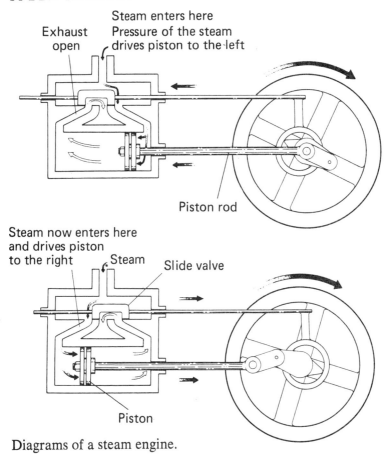

Diagrams of a steam engine.

The sled was accelerated by rockets for a distance of ½ mile during a period of 5 seconds. Then the sled coasted at a record speed for ½ second and was braked to a complete stop in slightly more than 1 second. During the sudden stop, the rider's eyeballs were thrown against his eyelids so hard that he suffered two black eyes.

In another experiment, a chimpanzee rode in the sled at 1,295 mph (2,084 kph).

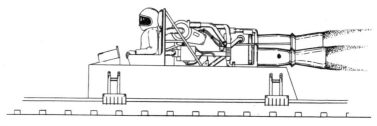

Man on a rocket sled.

From the Stanley Steamer to the Blue Flame

A steam engine was used in the first automobile to travel faster than a train. This was the Stanley Steamer, an American car which was driven at 150 mph in 1907. The development of steam cars had been delayed by opposition from the operators of railroads, since it was realized that cars would be a successful rival to railroads. In England there was a nineteenth-century law which limited the speed of steam cars to 4 mph on country roads and to 2 mph on roads in a town. The law also required a signalman to walk in front of a steam car to warn of its approach.

Steam cars never became popular because many people were afraid to drive a vehicle that had an open flame and hot steam. Also, the boilers generated steam too slowly for long-distance travel.

The electric car was most popular about 1900. They were easy to operate, ran quietly, and gave off no smelly fumes. But few of them could travel faster than 20 mph and their batteries needed charging about every 50 miles (80 kilometers).

The gasoline-powered car gradually replaced steam and electric cars. This type of engine, known as an *internal-combustion engine,* was developed in Europe. The automobile industry grew slowly until 1901. In that year there was a sharp drop in the price of gasoline. At the same time, the mass-production method of automobile manufacture was introduced.

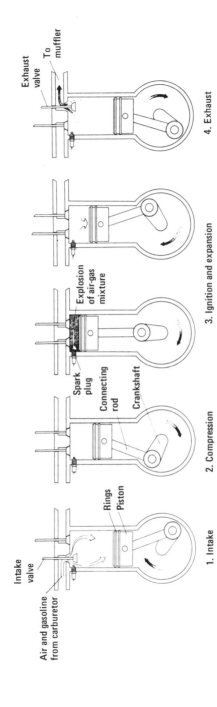

Diagrams of an internal-combustion engine cycle.

The first auto races were held in France in 1894. The winning cars averaged 15 mph. The Indianapolis 500 Race was first held in 1911. Table C shows how the Indianapolis course speed has increased since then.

TABLE C: *Winning speed of Indianapolis 500 at ten-year intervals.*

Year	Speed of winner (mph)
1911	75
1921	90
1931	97
1941	115
1951	126
1961	139
1971	157

At first, the main way to increase a racing car's speed was to make a bigger engine. Most early racers were therefore big and bulky. But new engines developed during World War I (1914–18) were smaller yet more powerful. This allowed racing cars in the 1920s and 1930s to be made trimmer and faster. During the 1960s racing engines were placed in the rear of cars.

Major changes were also made in the shape of racing cars. A surprising amount of air resistance is encountered at high speeds. Early racers were steamlined with slanted windshields and rounded hoods. A modern racing car is more like a narrow wedge, somewhat like the cross section of an airplane wing. As air passes over the top of the car, the car tends to lift slightly and loose contact with the pavement. The airfoil over the rear wheels is set at an angle to cause the air to push down and keep the car from rising.

Special cars are designed for breaking speed records. Many records have been set at the Bonneville Salt Flats in Utah. It was here that the world speed record for a piston-engined car was set in 1965, when Robert Summers traveled 418.504

mph. His car was 32 feet (9.8 meters) long and had four
Chrysler engines totaling 2,400 horsepower.

The highest ground speed attained by any wheeled vehicle
is 631.368 mph (1,016 kph), reached in 1970. Driving the
Blue Flame was Gary Gabelich. This car had a rocket engine
that burned liquid natural gas and hydrogen peroxide. At one
instant during the trials Gabelich was going 650 mph. In only
sixty-seven years automobile speeds had increased by over
500 mph.

It was at Bonneville Salt Flats, too, that the world's longest
skid occurred. In 1964 a jet-powered car went out of control
and skidded nearly 6 miles. The longest skid on a public road
was recorded in England in 1960, when a Jaguar had an accident and skidded 950 feet (285 meters). The longest bicycle

A speed car on the Bonneville Salt Flats, Utah. *Courtesy of
the Goodyear Motor Sports Club*

skid known to the authors is one of 44.5 feet, accomplished by Dean Smith, of Lincoln, Massachusetts, during a Boy Scout Bicycle Derby in 1977.

The speed record for a motorcycle on a race track is 182 mph (293 kph). This was set by a Kawasaki racer with a 748-cubic centimeter (cc) engine. A special speed motorcycle, 21 feet (6.4 meters) long went 286 mph (458 kph).

The fastest snowmobile traveled 115 mph (185 kph).

Airplanes and rockets

Once airplanes had been invented, it was possible for man to travel much faster than he could before on water or over land. The Wright brothers flew their first successful plane in 1903 at a speed of nearly 10 mph. By 1912 planes were being

A modern experimental speed plane. *Courtesy of Bell Aerospace*

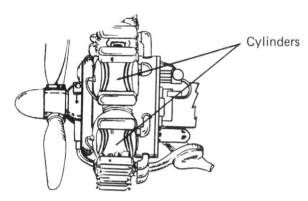

Cylinders

Propeller air propulsion.

built which flew more than 100 mph, and most people doubted that anyone would ever fly much faster. But during World War I fighter planes exceeded 150 mph, the land-speed record of the Stanley Steamer. However, these early planes could fly faster than that only during steep dives. By 1932 James Doolittle was winning races at speeds close to 300 mph. The record speed for a propeller-driven airplane now stands at 545 mph (877 kph).

When jet-powered aircraft were built, speed records took another big jump. During the Korean War (1950–54), the United States directed a major effort in perfecting jet propulsion in military planes. From 1951 to 1953, the Douglas Skyrocket plane made seven successive speed records, the last being 1,328 mph. By 1956 the Bell X-2 plane had sped 2,094 mph. Finally, after breaking the Bell record three times, a North American X-15 flew at 2,905 mph in 1961. More recently, an experimental rocket plane went 4,520 mph (7,273 kph).

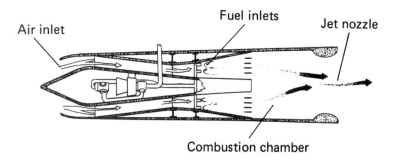

Jet air propulsion.

Airplane speeds are often compared with the speed of sound, which travels at about 750 mph (1,200 kph), or at Mach 1. The *Mach number* expresses the ratio between the speed of an object and the speed of sound. *Supersonic* means going faster than sound; any airplane going faster than Mach 1 is therefore flying at supersonic speed. An airplane going at Mach 2 would be traveling about 1,500 mph.

Air resistance at supersonic speeds becomes so intense that it makes an airplane hot. Flying at Mach 2, a plane attains a surface temperature of about 212° Fahrenheit (100° Celsius). At Mach 3 temperatures go up to 500° F. and at Mach 4 (3,000 mph) to 1,000° F. Naturally, special metals must be used so that a plane's exterior surfaces can withstand such high temperatures.

Present commercial jet liners have a top speed of about 625 mph (1,000 kph), but normally they cruise at about 550 mph (885 kph). Supersonic airplanes such as the British-French Concorde can fly at Mach 2—more than 1,500 mph (2,400 kph).

The helicopter speed record is only 266 mph (428 kph).

Of course, space rockets are man's fastest vehicles to date. It takes many minutes for a rocket to build up enough speed to escape the earth's gravity, but once the rocket is in space, there is no air to retard its flight. Space travel is also made

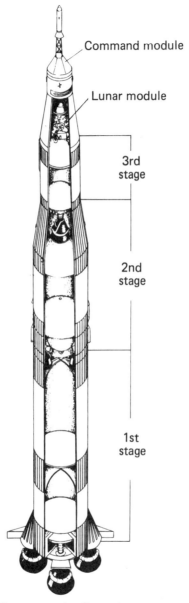

Command module

Lunar module

3rd
stage

2nd
stage

1st
stage

Three-stage Apollo rocket

Rocket air propulsion.

easier by the reduction of the earth's gravitational pull as the ship moves farther from earth.

Three United States spacemen hold today's ultimate speed record: Colonel Thomas P. Stafford, Commander Eugene A. Cernan, and Commander John W. Young. At one time during their Apollo 10 mission to the moon, they traveled at 24,791 mph (39,889 kph). This is more than 68 miles (109 kilometers) per second. How long would it take you to get to school at this speed?

Nature's records

Compared to man's space-travel flights, Mother Nature's records seem awfully slow. The fastest rapids ever navigated are on the Colorado River, in the Southwest. During floods, these white waters tumble along at 30 mph. While most ocean waves travel quite slowly, tidal waves caused by underwater earthquakes have been known to move at almost 500 mph (800 kph).

Natural wind speeds are nowhere near as great as that. Hurricane winds range between 75 to 120 mph. The highest recorded wind speed occurred on the summit of Mt. Washington, in New Hampshire, on April 12, 1934; one great gust blew at 231 mph (372 kph). Kite flying, anyone?

Wind speed is measured with an instrument called an *anemometer* (from *anemos,* the Greek word for wind). A small electric generator is attached to the bottom of a shaft supporting four cups. When the cups turn, the generator produces an electric current which moves the needle on a meter gauge. The faster the cups turn the stronger the electric current created. The meter can be calibrated to read the wind speed in mph or kph.

Speedometers

You are familiar with the speedometer in an automobile. The parts behind the dashboard are connected to the car's

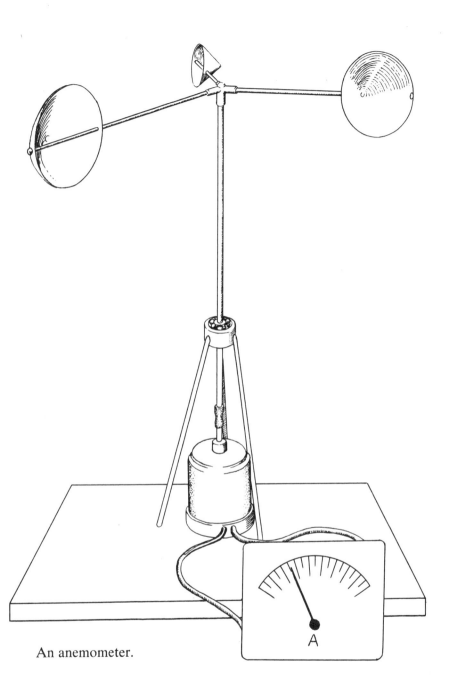

An anemometer.

drive shaft by a flexible cable. The speed shown by the speed-ometer needle is therefore actually governed by how fast the drive shaft turns. Have you ever noticed the speedometer when a car's wheels are spinning on ice? It might read 30 or 40 mph even though the car is barely moving.

A car speedometer cannot be made perfectly accurate. Tires become slightly smaller as they get worn. Since a smaller tire spins around a little faster than a larger one, the speedometer of a car with worn tires will probably read fast. If the car was moving at 40 mph, the speedometer might in-dicate 41 or 42 mph.

You can easily check the accuracy of your car's speedom-eter when traveling on a turnpike. Many interstate roads have markers to show each mile. At 50 mph, your car should take exactly 72 seconds to go 1 mile. Ask the driver to keep the car at 50 mph as you do the timing with a watch. The fact is that it takes most cars about 74 or 76 seconds to travel 1 mile when the speedometer reads 50. What does this mean?

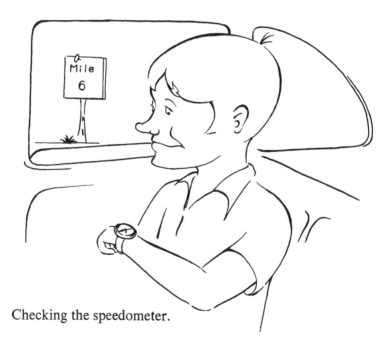

Checking the speedometer.

A boat speedometer is connected to a *Pitot tube* on the bottom of the boat that points toward the bow. As the boat moves, water is pushed into the tube and squeezes the air inside against a small bellows behind the dashboard. The minute movements of the bellows are magnified by levers and gears which are connected to the speedometer needle.

An airplane's speed is measured in a similar manner. Projecting from a wing is a *Pitot tube,* which leads to a bellows behind the instrument panel. The pressure of the *ram air* is an indication of the plane's speed. The problem with air is that its density (thickness) changes radically at different temperatures and altitudes. The thin air in the upper atmosphere would not push as hard on the bellows. To compensate for air changes, another device samples the temperature and pressure of the air outside the plane. These measurements are automatically converted into a ground-speed reading on the speedometer dial.

When speed records are being measured, more accurate instruments are required. The distance traveled is first measured precisely with surveying instruments. Electronic stopwatches are used to record the exact time for a vehicle to travel over the set course. Speed can then be computed from these figures.

Speed equals distance divided by time

As you probably know, speed is not a simple measurement like time or distance. Rather it is a combination of the two. To know any speed, you need a measurement of both time and distance. For car travel, it is convenient to use miles and hours. Other units are better for expressing slower speeds. For example, the movement of a glacier is often given in feet per year. A fast-moving glacier travels about 200 feet (61 meters) each year. This would be about 0.0000043 mph, which is too small a number to be easily understood. Rapid speeds require other units. Light travels some 186,000 miles

(300,000 kilometers) per second. Airplane and ship speeds are often expressed in *knots;* 1 knot is a little more than 1 mph.

Police use *radar* to measure automobile speeds. Continuous radio waves are directed at an approaching car. The waves are reflected from the car and sent back to the radar unit in the police cruiser. As the car gets closer, the time for the radar waves to return becomes shorter. Instruments analyze the changing times for the echoing waves to return and automatically compute the car's speed.

You can measure a car's speed quite accurately by marking a distance of 100 yards on the side of a road. When a car goes by, time it to see how long it takes for the car to travel between the two points. Use the table on page 21 to find out the car's speed.

Measuring a car's speed.

TABLE D: *Converting car time in mph.*

Time in seconds to travel 100 yards	Speed in mph
41	5
20	10
14	15
10	20
8	25
7	30
6	35
5	40
4½	45
4	50
3¾	55

A change in speed is known as *acceleration.* The lines on Graph A illustrate the acceleration of a skydiver after he jumps from the plane. The skydiver's terminal speed is about

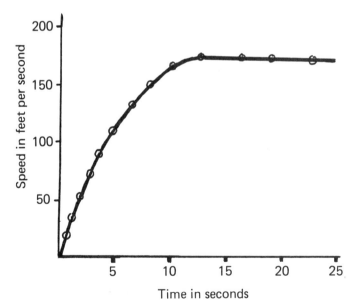

A skydiver's acceleration.

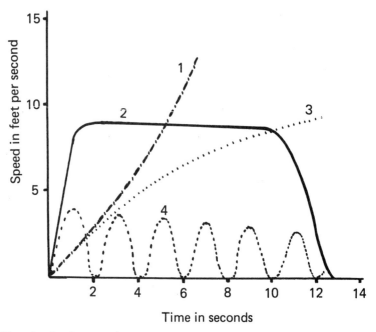

Graph of other motions.

170 feet per second, or 120 mph (193 kph), which occurs
after he has fallen for about 12 seconds. What change occurs
in the graph at this point?

Graph B has lines to show four other motions. Which line
best represents the motion of an elevator? Which one illus-
trates your motion on a swing?

II
Human Speeds

How fast do you run at top speed? Do you think that you can move faster than 15 mph (24 kph)? To find out, you can measure how long it takes you to run a certain distance.

One hundred yards is a good length. Measure this off on a level stretch of ground with a yardstick or carpenter's rule. Mark each end of the distance with a stick or small rock. You will need a friend to time you with a wristwatch or, even better, with a stopwatch. Try it several times to get your best time.

If you are good in math, you can compute your speed by using this formula:

$$\text{Speed in miles per hour (mph)} = \frac{205}{\text{time to run 100 yards}}$$

Or you can use Table E on the next page.

You can check your speed with a bicycle speedometer, also. Ask a friend to ride his bike beside you as you run. The rider should adjust his speed to keep the bike even with you. He can tell you your speed as it registers on the bike's speedometer.

The 100-yard dash

Some years ago a 10-second time for the 100-yard dash was a respectable track meet speed. Now, however, the world record is 9.0 seconds set by Ivory Crockett in 1974. His top speed toward the end of the race was 27.9 mph.

TABLE E: *Converting time into speed.*

Time in seconds to run 100 yards	Speed in mph	Speed in kph
10	20.5	32.8
10½	19.5	31.2
11	18.6	29.8
11½	17.8	28.5
12	17.1	27.4
12½	16.4	26.2
13	15.8	25.3
13½	15.2	24.3
14	14.6	23.4
14½	14.1	22.6
15	13.7	21.9
15½	13.2	21.1
16	12.8	20.5
16½	12.4	19.8
17	12.1	19.4

Short races are mainly a test of muscle strength and muscle speed; stamina is not required as it is in longer runs. It takes a runner 5 to 6 seconds to reach his full speed. By this time he has already gone more than halfway in the 100-yard dash. The runner can continue at top speed only until the 80- or 85-yard mark. Then, as his muscles tire, he slows down until crossing the finish line.

Table F shows the current record times for races of three other distances. Notice how the average speed changes as the length of the race increases.

The mile run

The mile has always been one of the most exciting track events. The first well-known miler was Walter George of England. When he ran a mile in 4 minutes 20 seconds in 1882, the event was hailed throughout the world. Four years later he

TABLE F: *Record times for short races.*

Distance	Runner	Year	Time	Speed
220 yd (⅛ mi)	T. Smith	1966	19.5 sec	23.1 mph
440 yd (¼ mi)	John Smith	1972	44.5 sec	20.2 mph
880 yd (½ mi)	R. Wohlhuter	1974	1 min.	
			43.9 sec	17.3 mph

cut his own time to 4:18 (4 minutes 18 seconds). The next great miler was Paavo Nurmi from Finland, who ran the mile in 4 minutes 10 seconds (4:10) in 1923. In 1935 Glenn Cunningham, one of America's greatest milers, ran an indoor mile in 4 minutes 4.4 seconds (4:4.4). At this time, few people felt the mile could ever be run in 4 minutes. But in the 1940s, two Swedish runners covered the distance in slightly more than 4 minutes 1 second (4:01).

Runners continued to strive for a 4-minute mile, but none succeeded until 1954, when Roger Bannister ran it in 3:59.4. Bannister's record lasted only a month. By 1962, a 4-minute mile had been run some seventy times by over thirty men. What was once thought impossible now seemed almost easy. The present record, set by John Walker of New Zealand, stands at 3:49.4.

It is strange that the 4-minute mile is now so common after never having been done for so many years. Part of the reason is because better training diets and more efficient conditioning techniques for runners have been developed by track coaches. Many other little things, though, such as improved track surfaces and even modern running shoes, have helped. But the psychological effect may be the most important of all. As soon as one man broke the 4-minute-mile barrier, it proved to other runners that the feat was no longer impossible.

The 4-minute mile was run outdoors more than fifty times before anyone could do it indoors. Races on indoor tracks are always slightly slower than outdoor races. This is partly because indoor tracks are built with wood and are harder to run on than the cinder surfaces used outdoors. Also, smaller indoor tracks require a runner to make more turns.

Longer running races

Olympic races are measured in meters. The 100-meter dash is run instead of the 100-yard dash. A meter is a little longer than a yard and 100 meters equal a little more than 109 yards. Table G shows the current world records for various distances. Can you explain why the speed for the 200-meter run is slightly greater than the 100-meter speed?

Ten thousand meters is equal to about 6.2 miles. Races of such length involve a lot more than the strength and speed of leg muscles. Runners must develop the stamina necessary to continue running long after the point at which an untrained man would drop from exhaustion. Breathing is of the greatest importance since working muscles require an abundant supply of oxygen.

The same men who win short races could never do well in long-distance races, nor could long-distance runners win sprints. Often a runner trains to excel just at one distance.

Swimming speed

The human body is not well adapted for swimming. But we do pretty well even without fins or webbed feet.

Swimming is a relatively new competitive sport. The first world swimming record was not recognized until 1878, when someone swam 100 yards in 68½ seconds. Early swimmers swam with a peculiar stroke with the arms and legs kept completely underwater. It was the Englishman John Trudgen in the 1890s who introduced the idea of lifting the arms *above* the surface of the water.

Not until 1905 did the first American swim 100 yards in 60 seconds. An average time in today's competitions for the 100-yard freestyle is 50 seconds, or a little over 4 mph.

TABLE G: *World records for Olympic running events.*

Event	Runner	Nationality	Year	Time	Speed in mph
100 meters	Jim Hines	U.S.A.	1968	9.9	22.8
200 meters	Tommie Smith	U.S.A.	1966	19.5	23.2
400 meters	Lee Evans	U.S.A.	1968	43.8	20.6
800 meters	Alberto Juan Torena	Cuba	1976	1:43.5	17.4
1,000 meters	Rick Wohlhuter	U.S.A.	1974	2:13.9	17.1
1,500 meters	Filbert Bayi	Tanzania	1974	3:32.2	16.0
5,000 meters	Emiel Puttemans	Belgium	1972	13:13	14.2
10,000 meters	Dave Bedford	Great Britain	1973	27:30.8	13.7

Speed over snow and ice

Man learned a long time ago that travel over snow was easier and faster on skis or sleds. As early as 3000 B.C. Scandinavians are thought to have been skiing faster than 35 mph. The current ski speed record is 109 mph achieved in Chile on a 62-degree slope. The bobsled record is 80 mph.

Skaters cannot go as fast as skiers, since they cannot take advantage of gravity. An ice hockey player skated close to 30 mph over a short distance while the fastest roller skater went 26 mph.

Iceboats can sail across a frozen lake faster than the wind. The record speed for an iceboat is 143 mph. It is possible to attain a speed of 140 mph in a wind of only 70 mph.

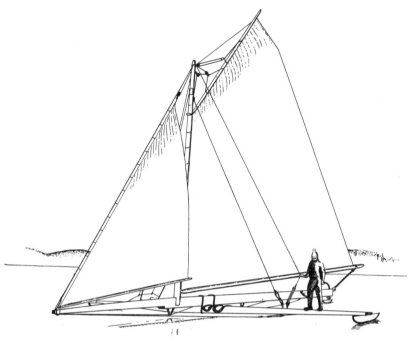

An iceboat.

Bicycle gears

The bicycle is one of the most efficient forms of self-locomotion. It takes practically no effort to propel yourself at a good speed over level ground.

The bicycle's power and speed advantage comes from its gears. The pedals are fixed to one large gear called the *sprocket gear*. One or more gears are mounted on the hub of the rear wheel. The size of the gears determines how much power or speed is delivered to the rear wheels when the rider is pedaling.

Three different sets of gears are shown in the illustration. Gear A has the same number of teeth as Gear B. Here the wheel and the pedals would turn at exactly the same speed. Gear C, however, has half as many teeth as Gear D. The

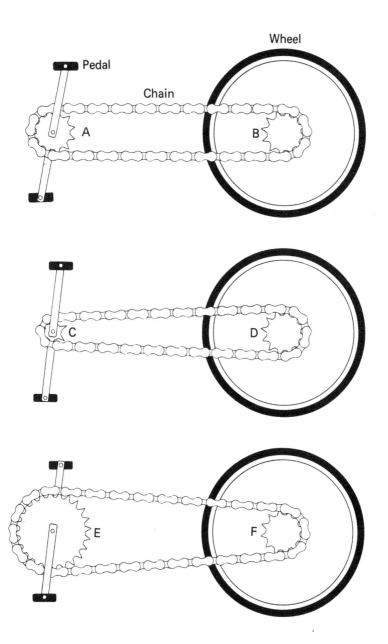

Gear arrangements.

smaller gear would have to be turned twice in order to make the larger gear on the wheel go around once. And Gear E has twice as many teeth as Gear F. If Gear E turns once, how many times would the wheel go around?

"Low gear" is used for starting or pumping up a hill. When you need more power, the gear on the wheel should be a lot smaller than the sprocket gear. On level ground at high speed, you should use "high gear." Now the wheel gear is almost as large as the sprocket gear. Notice that you do not get both more power *and* more speed; you can only get either one or the other. The less speed you have, the more power you get. And with increased speed you lose power.

Old bikes had just one gear on the rear-wheel hub. Modern ten-speed bikes have five gears on the wheel and two on the sprocket. The ten different "speeds" are made by switching the chain around to give ten different gear combinations. Of course, you can change your speed in one gear just by pedaling faster or slower, but a "ten-speed bike" means one which can have ten different gear arrangements.

Here is how you can find out about the gears on your bike. Turn your bike upside down so it rests on the seat and handle bars. Turn the pedals slowly, counting how many turns the rear wheel makes for each five turns of the pedal. It helps to have a friend count the wheel turns while you turn the pedal. You might want to record your results in a table such as the one below.

TABLE H: *Bicycle gear ratios.*

Sprocket gear	Rear-wheel gear	Number of turns rear wheel makes for five turns of the sprocket gear
52 teeth	14 teeth	18½
52	17	15
52	21	12½
52	26	10
52	32	8

Checking the number of wheel turns.

Another way to do this is to pedal your bike in each gear. Use the lowest gear first and ride over a certain distance. Count the number of complete turns your feet make during the trip. You cannot do any coasting; you must pedal all the way. Travel the same route again in the other gears, counting the number of pedal turns each time. Why do your feet go more slowly when you pedal in high gear?

The record speed for a bicycle race over a short distance is 42 mph. The fastest bike rider was a Frenchman who pedaled 127 mph. But he was riding just behind a special windshield attached to a race car.

Riding a bike fast may be fun, but it is quite dangerous. You can get badly hurt if you fall off your bike. Always ride carefully; never speed.

The fast ball

How fast is a baseball pitcher's fast ball? Pitchers wondered for a long time, since there was no way to measure the ball's speed. It appeared to travel the 60 feet from the pitcher to the

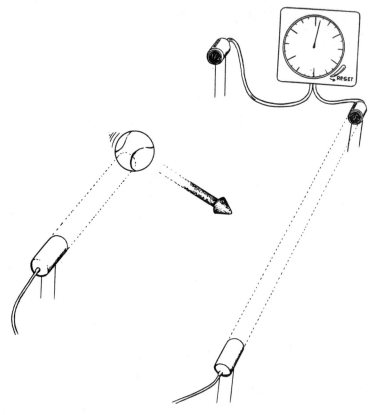

Schematic drawing of an electronic timer timing a baseball's speed.

catcher in about 1 second. Stopwatches were no good for measuring such short times because a person could not start or stop the watch accurately. More precise timing devices had to be invented before the speed of a fast ball could be determined.

Modern electronic timers are accurate to within $\frac{1}{1000}$ of a second. They utilize two photocells to start and stop a special timing device. A beam of light is directed at the photocell. When an object passes in front of the light, a shadow is cast on the photocell. The cell then automatically closes or opens a switch, which in turn starts or stops the timer.

Table I shows the top speed for three different balls and an ice hockey puck. A ball begins to slow down immediately after it is hit or thrown because of air resistance. A Ping-Pong ball is so light that it travels less than 30 feet even when slammed at 60 mph. A golf ball goes faster than most other balls. It is small and heavy, and the leverage of the golf club magnifies the force of the golfer's arms.

TABLE I: *Ball speeds.*

Object	Top speed (mph)
Ping-Pong ball (slammed)	60
Baseball (pitched)	101
Hockey puck (slap shot)	118
Golf ball (drive)	170

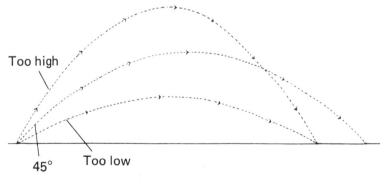

Three baseball flight-path trajectories.

The distance a ball travels provides a rough idea of its speed. A baseball can be hit with a bat more than twice as far as it can be thrown, which indicates that a batted baseball has a greater speed than a thrown ball. Of course, the ball's angle of travel also influences its distance. The greatest distance can be reached if you hit it into the air at an angle of 45 degrees above the ground.

Here is a list of some other things you can throw or hit. Which of these do you think goes the fastest?

1. Served tennis ball.
2. Arrow shot from a bow.
3. Kicked soccer ball.
4. Passed football.
5. Thrown Frisbee.

How fast can you throw?

You can find the speed of a ball by throwing it straight up into the air. The faster you throw, the longer the ball stays up.

You will need a friend to help you time it. A stopwatch is more accurate, but a wristwatch with a sweep second hand will be all right. Throw a baseball as hard as you can straight up over your head. As you release the ball, say "Start," so the timer knows when to begin. When the ball strikes the ground, shout "Stop." Try it four or five times.

Here is the formula for computing speed from the time the ball stays in the air:

Speed in feet per second $= 16 \times$ time in air in seconds.

Or you can use Table J to convert your times into speeds in miles per hour.

Measuring a baseball's speed.

TABLE J: *Changing ball air time into speed.*

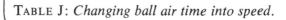

Time in seconds ball stays in air	Mph
2	22
2½	28
3	32
3½	38
4	44
4½	48
5	54
5½	60
6	66

III

Animal Locomotion

Fish swimming speeds

Animals first moved in the warm waters of prehistoric oceans. Before this, more primitive animals merely drifted about in the current with no means to control their place in the world. Through gradual adaptations, some creatures began to wiggle in just the right way to move. Such animals could now escape from enemies and harsh environments as well as seek food. They had bridged a basic gap between plants and animals: mobility.

Unlike humans, fishes are beautifully adapted for swimming. The bodies of most fish are rounded and sleek—the perfect shape for slipping through water with minimum resistance. As the streamlined fish body moves forward, water

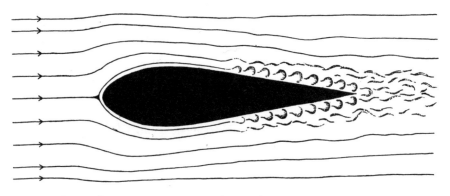

Water flow around a streamlined shape.

Trout

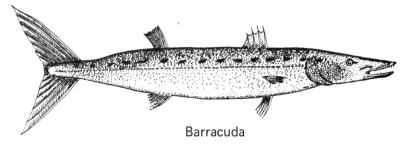

Barracuda

Structure of a slow swimmer (trout) compared with a fast swimmer (barracuda).

flows smoothly over its front and sides. Toward the tail, however, the water becomes swirling and *turbulent*. Almost all of the fast-swimming fish have a forked tail, like that of the barracuda in the illustration. Notice that such an arrangement prevents the tail from dragging in the turbulent water left behind.

Motorboats move in a completely different way than fish. The boat propeller turns on a shaft in a continuous rotary movement. Such a motion could never be made by a fish, since all parts of an animal must be supplied with nerves and blood vessels. There is no way that blood could be sent to a tail spinning around and around. The vessels would be severed by the rotation.

A fish swims by sweeping its tail back and forth, pushing against the water. The bones in the fish's spine are hinged with smooth joints, permitting its tail to operate as a flexible lever. The contraction of the powerful body muscles whip the tail rapidly from side to side, driving the fish forward.

Scientists have experimented to find out if a fish's tail motion is as efficient as the steadily turning screw propellers of a ship. In order to find out, they need to measure how fast fish swim.

Fish do not swim as fast as most people think. To a fisherman, the startled trout appears to dart off at a high speed. But the human eye is a poor judge of sudden movement.

There is a shortage of reliable data on the swimming speed of fish. Most scientific measurements have been made in the

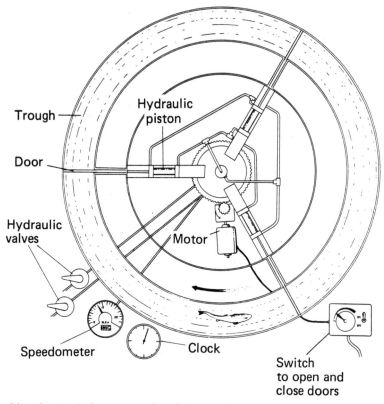

Circular tank for measuring fish speed.

laboratory on small fish. The speeds may not be accurate because laboratory fish are often in a weak condition and do not behave as they do in their natural habitat.

Some speed measurements have been done with a camera. A more complicated apparatus is pictured here. The fish swims in the circular trough which is rotated by an electric motor. The speed of the trough is adjusted so that the swimming fish appears stationary. The speed of the fish is then indicated on the speedometer. The three doors make the water move at the same speed as the trough. Each door is opened in time to let the fish swim through.

It was found that a small fish can move about ten times the length of its body each second. Most large fish can swim faster than small ones. Table K shows the maximum observed speeds for five kinds of fish. A brook trout 8 inches long swims 4 mph, while a foot-long trout can travel about 6½ mph. These speeds are really not very fast.

TABLE K: *Maximum fish speeds.*

Species	Length in inches	Maximum speed (mph)
Brook trout	8	4
	11	6½
Dace	7	4
	8	5½
Pike	6	4¾
	8	3¼
Goldfish	3	1½
	5	4
Barracuda	48	27

A fish's speed is related to the size of its tail and how rapidly that beats from side to side. At a 1½-inch trout's top speed of 1½ mph, its tail wiggles back and forth some twenty-four times per second. An 11-inch trout's tail beats 16 times a second, permitting it to move forward at 6½ mph.

A fish can move at top speed only briefly when frightened. For a fish, speed swimming for a long time is unimportant.

Short bursts of sudden speed are needed mainly for it to escape danger or to capture prey.

The speed of larger fish has been figured by less accurate means. The jumps of leaping salmon have been as high as 6 feet up and 12 feet forward through the air. Calculations have shown that a speed of 14 mph would be required for the fish to travel this distance out of water. Salmon can maintain only an 8 mph speed for any length of time. Each year salmon from the ocean swim back up rivers where they were spawned to lay their eggs and fertilize them. They are strong enough to swim up high waterfalls.

Unlike the fishes, which all have tails moving from side to side, the tails of dolphins and whales, which are marine mammals, go up and down. Since dolphins frequently swim along beside a boat, that they can attain speeds of about 22 mph has been known for a long time. Even the 90-foot blue whale can wallow through the ocean at 20 mph.

It is thought that a swordfish can swim almost 40 mph. This big fish occasionally drives its long bill into the wooden hull of a large boat. One swordfish bill penetrated a piece of timber 22 inches. Calculations show that the fish would have to be swimming 40 mph in order to do this.

The fastest fish known are the tuna and the sailfish. A fishing boat once clocked a bluefin tuna at 43 mph. The greatest swimmer of all is the sailfish, which probably can swim faster than 65 mph.

The horse

The first animal to walk on land was a fish. It was a kind of lobe-finned fish that used its fins like flippers to move slowly along the ground. Evolutionary changes, occurring over millions of years, brought about a salamanderlike amphibian with crude legs and feet. From these first land-dwelling vertebrates came the great variety of animals which now roam the earth by walking, hopping, and running.

The horse is one of the greatest runners. Before the "iron horse" (railroad) and the "horseless carriage" (automobile), horses provided the fastest and surest transportation on land. The early Greeks and Romans used battle horses to move soldiers quickly from place to place. Later, the English bred powerful war horses able to carry men wearing 400-pound (181-kilogram) suits of armor. There were no horses in North America when the Europeans arrived. After the Indians got horses left behind by the Spanish explorers, they used them to hunt buffalo and in battles against other tribes. For a little more than a year, riders of the Pony Express carried the fastest messages to the West, until the telegraph was completed in late 1861.

The horse gets its speed from four powerful legs. The long legs of all hoofed animals are partly the result of an "extra" leg bone. Your leg has two main bones, the thigh bone (femur) and the shin bone (tibia). The horse leg has a third long bone, the *cannon bone*. Since the cannon bone is really

A trotting-horse skeleton. *Courtesy of The American Museum of Natural History*

two elongated foot bones fused together, you can say that the
horse runs on its tiptoes.

The horse moves at three distinct natural speeds, or *gaits*.
The walk is about 4 mph. When walking, the horse raises one
foot at a time and places it down on the ground again before

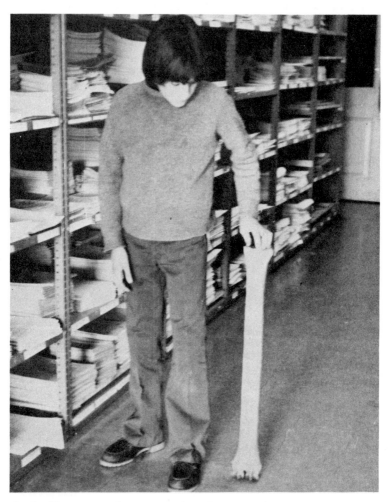

A giraffe cannon bone may be almost as long as your entire
leg. *David Webster Photo*

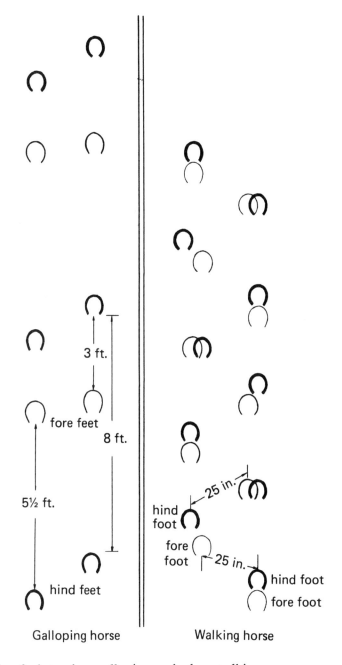

3 ft.

fore feet

8 ft.

5½ ft.

hind feet

hind foot

fore foot

25 in.

25 in.

hind foot

fore foot

Galloping horse

Walking horse

Horse hoofprints when galloping and when walking.

raising the next foot. The feet move in a regular order: right fore foot, left hind foot, left fore foot, and right hind foot. Horses trot at about 9 mph, with the front leg on one side of the body and the hind leg on the other side of the body hitting the ground together. The gallop is the horse's fastest gait. Galloping horses bound forward in mighty leaps by pulling their hind legs under their bodies and pushing out with great force. All four feet are off the ground at one point in each stride. Race horses can gallop 1 mile at more than 38 mph (61 kph).

Special legs and feet

The kangaroo is the mightiest jumper. Its hind foot has three toes, the center one being extra large and ending in a huge claw. The normal jump of a 200-pound (91-kilogram) kangaroo is a 5- to 10-foot hop. But when chased, the animal can cover 20 feet (6 meters) or more in a single bound.

The jack rabbit is another good jumper. It can hop 700

Do you think that this animal would run, walk, or hop? *Courtesy of Education Development Center Inc.*

yards (640 meters) in a minute, a speed of about 24 mph (38 kph).

The feet and legs of other animals have become adapted to traveling in different terrains. The cushioned feet of a camel help this desert dweller to walk on top of soft sand. Polar bears have feet with soles almost completely covered with hair to prevent them from slipping on ice. The front legs of the Rocky Mountain goat are shortened from the knee to the foot. They often use their front legs as a hook to hold on to the top of a rocky ledge after a jump. Squirrels have special climbing feet: needle-sharp claws and bumpy foot pads which may help them grip smooth surfaces. You probably have seen squirrels walking with ease along a slender branch or telephone wire.

Animal speeds

Some animals which appear to move quickly are actually quite slow. The fastest spider can run at only 1.2 mph, while a centipede can scurry away at 5 mph. Snakes just seem to travel fast because they wiggle so much. The fastest snake, the black mamba, can move at 7 mph.

One of the slowest animals is the giant tortoise, who lumbers along at only 0.17 mph. The slowest mammal is the ai, the three-toed sloth of tropical America. It has a top speed of 6 to 8 feet per minute, which is only 0.08 mph. But the snail's pace remains the slowest of all, 0.03 mph. At this rate, the snail could crawl 1 mile in thirty-three hours.

Horses and greyhounds run around a race track at almost the same speed. The fastest greyhound on record ran 42 mph, while the fastest race horse ran 43 mph (69 kph). The race horse would beat the dog even with a major disadvantage: it has to carry a saddle and a jockey on its back.

The best long-distance runner is the pronghorn antelope. This animal can run at 55 mph for a distance of ½ mile, and 42 mph for 1 mile. Even more impressive is its speed of 35 mph over a 4-mile run.

The champion animal runner is the cheetah. Most members

of the cat family rely on stealth to catch their food. They sneak up slowly on an unsuspecting animal until they are close enough to catch it in one great leap. The cheetah is an exception; this big cat chases its prey at full speed until one of them tires out. Over a short distance, the cheetah can run 60 to 63 mph (101 kph). This is usually fast enough to run down even the antelope.

Muscle pairs

The cheetah's running ability depends upon the strength and endurance of its leg muscles. Since a muscle can exert a force only when contracting, muscles almost always occur in pairs. Usually one muscle of a pair is stronger than the other. This is why you can kick your leg harder in a forward direction than you can kick backward.

You can use a bathroom scale to measure the strength of some of your muscle pairs. Sit on a chair and push your leg forward against a scale that is leaning against the wall. How hard can you push forward? Now stand the scale on end against one of the front legs of the chair. Pull your leg back so your heel is pressing against the scale. How hard can your muscles pull your leg backward?

Measure the strength of other muscle pairs. To do this, you will have to figure out how to place the scales. It would probably be easier if you had an assistant to help you hold the scale and then read it. You can keep track of your results in a table similar to the one shown on page 47.

Is one muscle in each pair always quite a lot stronger than the other muscle? Which is the strongest of all?

Muscles become temporarily weaker if they are used continuously. To see how much strength your finger muscles lose, hold a bathroom scale with one hand on either side and squeeze as hard as you can. Are you able to make the scale read more than 60 pounds (27 kilograms)? Put the scale down and open and close your fingers as fast as you can for a

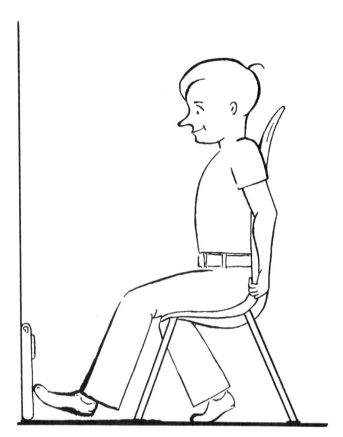

Testing one's leg muscles.

TABLE L: *Strength of muscle pairs.*

Muscles	Muscles used	Pounds
Lower leg	leg moving forward	
	leg moving backward	
Foot	toe pushing down	
	toe lifting up	
Fingers	squeezing together	
	pushing apart	
Lower arm	arm pushing down	
	arm lifting up	
Neck	head moving forward	
	head moving backward	

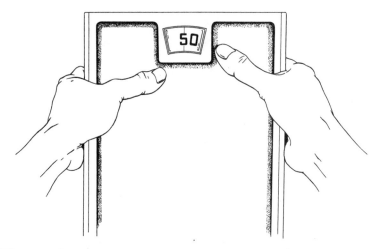

The muscle-exhaustion test.

minute or more. Then immediately squeeze the scale again. Are your fingers less than half as strong as before? How long does it take for the muscles to regain their original strength?

To fly like a bird

It was the flight of the birds that men always envied the most. While not as fast as the horse or antelope, men could run more swiftly than many animals. And they could swim better than almost any animal that did not live in the water. But fly? Never!

People first thought a pair of wings was all that was needed. There is an ancient Greek legend about two men who escape from prison with wings. Daedalus and his son, Icarus, fashioned wings of feathers set in beeswax. Daedalus showed his son how to use his pair of wings and warned him not to fly too high or the sun's heat would melt the wax. The two climbed the highest tower of their prison and flew away like two giant birds. Young Icarus became so excited with flying that he flew higher and higher toward the sun. The feathers came loose

The flight of Icarus and Daedalus.

when the wax melted, and the boy fell into the sea and drowned.

For thousands of years, men wasted their time trying to copy the birds. Their reasoning was simple enough. The tiny muscles of birds could lift them into the air with seeming ease. Surely man, with his much greater strength, could do at least as well.

Many men in centuries past really were able to glide with rigid wings. The delicate wings were carried to the top of a high hill. Then the flier would hold the glider over his head and run down the hill into the wind. If lucky, he might get airborne for a short distance. Often, though, the flier would get hurt when the glider went out of control and crashed.

Leonardo da Vinci, the great artist and inventor who lived at the time of Columbus, designed many wing structures. He realized that man did not have enough strength to fly using just his arm muscles. One plan had wings that were flapped by a combination of both arm and leg movement. Another plan used head motion to control the device's tail surfaces.

Other flight pioneers continued to try flapping wings strapped to their arms. Sometimes the wings were even made of bird feathers sewn together. The hopeful flier would jump from a cliff or tall building and then start flapping. Almost always these ridiculous-looking birdmen dropped straight to the ground.

Some of the first powered airplanes were designed as direct copies of birds. But success came only after an engine-powered propeller was used to drive a large glider. Men have long since mastered the design of aircraft driven with energy from fuels.

Muscle-powered flight, however, has been accomplished. The latest design for a muscle-driven craft is called the *Gossamer Condor*. This 70-pound (31.5-kilogram) plane was built largely of cardboard, aluminum tubes, and balsa wood and covered with plastic film. On August 23, 1977, the pilot (Bryan Allen) managed to fly a distance of 1.15 miles (1.84 kilometers) in 6 minutes 22½ seconds.

How birds do it

It takes more than wings to fly. Most birds possess the other prime requirements for flight: low weight and high power.

An animal's motion is dependent upon food. *Metabolism* is the complex chemical reaction within the body cells by which food is converted into the energy required for muscle movement. As with the burning of gasoline in a car's engine, oxygen from the air is an essential ingredient for this metabolic process. An additional product of metabolism is heat, used to maintain body temperature.

Since flying requires more energy than swimming or running, birds must possess an efficient digestive system. Their food is digested much more rapidly than that of most other animals. Food often passes through the bird's entire digestive tract in 1 hour, as compared with your 24 hours. Birds eat foods that are high in energy, such as seeds, fruits, worms, insects, rodents, and fish.

The bird's air supply is increased by five or more pairs of air sacs which extend through the body, some even filling hollow bones. These supplement air in its lungs for respiration and cooling.

Birds' blood circulation system, too, is designed for the rapid distribution of oxygen to the muscles. Birds' hearts are large and powerful and beat a lot more rapidly than those of

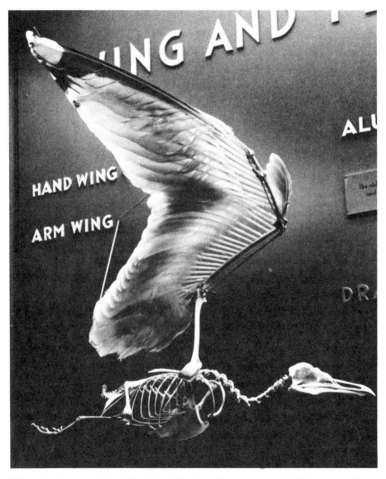

The skeleton of a bird in flight. *Courtesy of The American Museum of Natural History*

other animals. Their accelerated metabolism rate also means an increased body temperature, in some birds as high as 113° F. (45° C.).

The powerful muscles that move the bird's wings are located in its breast, rather than on the wings themselves. If the wings had muscles like your arms and legs, they would be much too heavy to flap up and down. The breast muscles are connected to the wing bones by extra long tendons. In a strong flier, such as a pigeon, these muscles may make up as much as half of its total body weight. Soaring birds, though, have reduced breast muscles and stronger wing tendons. Most of the time these gliding birds hold their wings out in a soaring position and float on air updrafts.

The skeleton on a bird is extremely light yet remarkably strong and elastic—characteristics which are necessary for an air frame subjected to stresses when flying. The bones are hollow and thin. The wing bones of some large soaring birds have internal braces, much like the trusses in a real airplane wing. Many other bones which occur separated in most animals are fused together in a bird to form a strong, light structure.

Another weight-saving feature is the bird's light head. A pigeon skull comprises only ⅕ of 1 per cent of its total body weight. Much weight is also saved by the elimination of teeth and the accompanying heavy jaws and jaw muscles.

By necessity, the largest bone the bird has is its breastbone, or *sternum*. The ridgelike *keel* along the bottom provides the large area needed for the attachment of the breast muscles that move the wings. Keel size is a good key to wing power: the larger the keel, the stronger the flier.

The bird's streamlined body is sleekly contoured with smooth feathers that reduce air friction and turbulence. There are no ears sticking out of its head. Most birds withdraw their legs when flying, just as the landing gear of modern aircraft is retracted after take-off.

Of all the bird's special structural modifications for flying, its feathers are unique. They are exceedingly light in weight, yet flexible and strong. No man-made structure can match the natural performance of a bird's feathered wing.

The bird does not need a propeller; its wings provide both lift and forward motion. The inner half of the wing is shaped much like the cross section of an airplane wing and provides lift in the same way. The bird's forward speed is produced by the large primary feathers on the outer half of each wing. As the wing is driven down, the broad trailing edges of the flexible feathers bend upward. These angled surfaces give the same forward force as the pitch on a spinning propeller blade of an airplane. On the upward stroke of the wings, the outer tips of the primary feathers separate and twist edgewise. If it was not for this "feathering" action, the upstrokes would cancel out the lifting gained by the downstroke.

Birds do more than just flap their wings up and down. Slow motion photography has shown that the wings are twisted so their outer tips move in a figure-eight path. As soaring birds glide, they make continual adjustments in the position of the wing tips. Without these slight changes, the bird would quickly drift off course.

Thanks to all their superb adaptations, birds can perform flight maneuvers that outshine man's best aircraft. An albatross can glide for hours on wings stretching 11 feet (3.4 meters). The hummingbird's tiny wings beat at sixty times a sec-

Start of downstroke   End of downstroke   Part way through upstroke

A bird's wings and feathers in three stages of flight.

ond, while it darts quickly in any direction or hangs motionlessly in the air. A golden plover loses only 2 ounces (0.36 kilogram) of weight during its seasonal migratory nonstop flight of 2,400 miles. Geese have been seen flying at a height of almost 6 miles (9.6 kilometers) above the earth. Some swifts fly at over 100 mph, and airplanes have followed diving hawks and eagles at 180 mph. And the awkward-looking owl can fly down and grab a running rabbit in absolute silence.

Of course, man's airplanes today can fly higher and farther and faster than any bird. But not without a lot more weight and fuel and noise. Nature has designed the bird to be the ultimate flying machine.

Now maybe you can understand why man will never fly without the aid of machines. He could easily manufacture a big pair of wings complete with artificial bones and tendons. But he would need the muscles of a superman to move the wings fast enough to fly. Man's body is too stout, his heart too weak, and his head too heavy. To fly like a bird, man must build flying machines that use the natural laws of motion.

IV

Experiments in Motion

The Moving-Right-Along Law—Part I

Imagine that you are on a motor trip crossing the flat plains of mid-America. Suddenly the car stops. It is out of gas!

"No problem," says the driver. "We'll give it a push to start it rolling. Then we can jump in and ride to the next gasoline station. The car will keep moving right along—it's a basic law of nature."

Of course, you wouldn't believe him! But, believe it or not, he's right in principle! Unfortunately, he's forgotten some details.

Now, really stretch your imagination! You are an astronaut out in space. You were fixing a jet on the outside of your spaceship when you let go. You find that you are drifting slowly away from the ship.

You turn on your radio and shout, "Help! I'm moving away from the ship!"

"Take it easy!" replies your commander. "Just throw the wrench you were using in a direction that points away from the ship. Throw it as hard as you can. It will make you move toward the ship. It's a basic law of nature."

You give it a try. Sure enough, it works! You begin moving back toward the ship.

The basic laws of nature that the driver and the spaceship commander were talking about were first discovered by the Pisan astronomer Galileo and the English mathematician Sir Isaac Newton over 300 years ago.

A space walk. *National Aeronautics and Space Administration Photo*

Many of the experiments that follow are similar to experiments they did. See if your results lead you to conclusions similar to theirs!

Experiment 1: Down a hill, up a hill

Place a long sheet of thin cardboard or poster board in a shallow box that is about as wide as the sheet. The photograph shows you how to make a mini-roller-coaster hill from these materials.

Let a marble or a light ball roll down the hill. What happens to its speed? What happens as it goes up the hill on the other side? Then what happens?

You will find that the marble returns to very nearly the height from which it started.

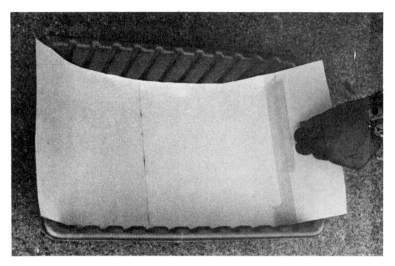

A sheet of cardboard in a shallow box. *Robert Gardner Photo*

Now make one side of the hill longer by making the side from which the ball starts shorter but steeper. Does the ball still return to very nearly the height from which it started? (Friction between the ball and the hill causes the ball eventually to stop.)

If there was no second hill but instead a *frictionless* level surface that extended forever, what would happen?

Experiment 2: A pendulum

Use a long piece of thread or string to suspend a pendulum bob (a steel washer, a lead fishing sinker, a stone, etc.) from a beam, the top of a doorway, a stairwell, a jungle gym, or some other high place. Fasten the upper end of the pendulum string to a hook, a thumb tack, or tape. Watch it swing for a while. What do you notice about the swinging pendulum?

Pull the bob a few centimeters to one side, place your nose just behind it and release it. Can you keep your nose in the same place without blinking as the bob swings back toward you?

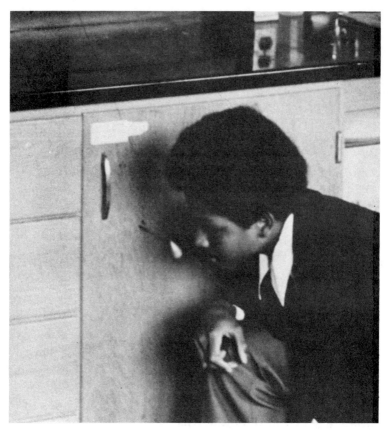

Try not to blink. *Robert Gardner Photo*

With a little practice, you can do it, but you may have to close your eyes. Above all, don't push the bob and don't move your head.

Does the pendulum bob reach your nose on its return swing? How long does the pendulum keep swinging? What finally makes it stop? Do you see how watching pendulums made Galileo believe that moving things tend to keep moving?

Experiment 3: Spin your wheels

Turn your bicycle upside down and give the front wheel a good pull. If the bearings are good, the wheel will continue turning for a long time. What would happen if the bearings were frictionless?

Try spinning a turntable, a lazy susan, a playground merry-go-round, a top, or a small gyroscope. Why do some of these objects keep spinning longer than others?

Experiment 4: A caged marble

The things you spun in Experiment 3 could only go in circles. But suppose you have something moving round and

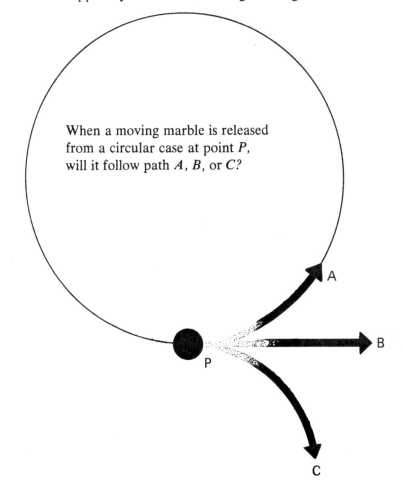

When a moving marble is released from a circular case at point *P*, will it follow path *A*, *B*, or *C?*

round and you remove the force that makes it go in a circle. Will it continue to circle or will it move in another direction?

To find out, place a marble or a small ball under a clear circular dish such as a cake cover. By moving the dish quickly in small circles, you can get the marble to move around the inside circumference of the dish. Where will the marble go if you suddenly lift one side of the dish? Which of the paths in the drawing best describes the marble's path?

Experiment 5: An air car

You found in Experiment 4 that an object moving in a circle will move along path B when you remove the force that makes it follow a circular path.

To see if it moves at a *constant speed* along a straight line, you need to reduce friction as much as possible. To do this, you can build a "car" that floats on a thin layer of air. It's quite easy to make one!

Air car: parts (right) and assembled model. *Robert Gardner Photo*

Drill a $\frac{1}{16}$-inch (1½-millimeter) hole in the center of a piece of ¼-inch- (3-millimeter-) thick plywood or Masonite. The thin piece of wood can be either a square about 2½ inches (6–7 centimeters) on a side or a circle with a similar diameter.

Use sandpaper to make one side of the wood very smooth. Be sure the edges are sanded too. If the piece of wood is square, the corners should be rounded off a little so they will not hinder the "car" in its motion.

Next, glue the flat end of a wooden spool (there may be one in your home sewing kit) or a cork with a hole through it to the unsanded side of the square or disc. Be sure the hole in the spool is right over the hole in the wood.

After the glue is dry, attach an inflated balloon to the spool. (You may want to tie off the neck of the balloon while you connect it to the spool.) Slide the air car along a smooth level surface such as a formica-covered counter or table. Does the car show any sign of slowing down?

In addition to these experiments, you feel, do, and see things in your daily life that shed light on the nature of motion. Some of the things you experience were unknown to Galileo. With which of the experiences below would Galileo have been familiar?

When you are on a seesaw, notice how you keep going up after your partner's end of the board hits the ground. Or feel the bump you get because you tend to keep going after your end of the seesaw hits the ground.

You have probably noticed that you tend to keep moving when an automobile, a train, or a subway comes to a sudden stop. In an automobile you feel the seat belt holding you back when this happens. That's why seat belts are so helpful in preventing injuries. They keep you from hitting the dashboard, windshield or the back of the front seat when a car stops suddenly or bumps into something.

When highways are icy, cars sometimes slide off the road as they try to go around a corner. The ice prevents the tires from gripping the road so the car continues along a straight line because it cannot get any force to change its direction. (Remember Experiment 4!)

Galileo said that *objects in motion continue to move in a straight line at constant speed when no force acts on them.* On earth, friction and the force of gravity prevent us from seeing Galileo's idea in the manner that he imagined it. To get a sense of his idea in its purest form, close your eyes and imagine that you are in a spaceship. The ship is so far away from the earth, other planets, or stars that there is no gravity. With nothing pulling on it, the ship moves in a straight line at constant speed. It moves silently with its jet engines off. Inside you float around in a weightless condition. Nothing holds you to the floor or to the ceiling. There is no up or down. To move about you have to push or pull on things within the ship. It would be a strange place to live, but you would know exactly what Galileo meant.

The Moving-Right-Along Law—Part II

The tendency of an object to maintain its state of motion is called *inertia.* You've seen that something in motion tends to keep moving. But what if an object is at rest? Will it tend to stay at rest at a constant speed of *zero?*

Here are some experiments that will help you to answer that question.

Experiment 6: Coin, card, and cup

Place a file card or playing card over the open end of a drinking glass or a cup. Put a coin on the center of the card. Snap your finger against one edge of the card to shoot it off the glass. What happens to the coin? Does it tend to remain at rest?

Now place the card on the edge of a table so that about one third of the card extends beyond the edge. Put some water in a glass or cup and place it on the other two thirds of the card.

Give the card a quick jerk toward you. What happens to the glass? Does it tend to remain at rest?

Once you are confident that things do tend to stay in place, you may want to try a trick you have probably seen in a movie or on TV. Cover a small table or counter with a smooth cloth or a newspaper. Put a plate, a cup and saucer, and a glass of water on the cloth. With a sharp yank you can pull the cloth out from the utensils, leaving them undisturbed on the table. (It's a good idea to use unbreakable dishes until you are an expert in this experiment.)

Experiment 7: Karate chop

Place a thin stick about 12–18 inches (30–50 centimeters) long on a table. Let one half the stick extend beyond the edge of the table. Cover the other half with a newspaper. Give the uncovered half of the stick a sharp blow with a heavy stick or a baseball bat. Does the stick break or does the paper flip off the table? Why?

Do objects at rest tend to remain at rest?

Experiment 8: Spinning eggs

Take two eggs. One must be hard-boiled, the other uncooked. Place the hard-boiled egg on its side on a table top and spin the egg. Stop it for a moment, then let go. Repeat the experiment with the uncooked egg.

Which egg will start to spin again after it has been stopped? Why?

The results of this experiment are similar to what happens to you when a car or train in which you are riding suddenly stops. You continue to move just as the liquid in the uncooked egg did. If a seat belt holds you firmly in place, you stop with the car just as the hard-boiled contents of the egg stopped when the shell stopped.

Galileo said that things keep moving *if no force acts on them*. Usually there is a force—a force that we call *friction*. What Galileo did was to *imagine* what would happen *if* there were no friction, just as you imagined what would happen in a spaceship far out in space.

Galileo also thought about the many things that do seem to keep moving right along. The stars, moon, and sun, for instance, seem to move at steady speeds about a motionless earth. Despite what others said, Galileo believed that the earth turned constantly about its axis making the heavens appear to rotate. If not, then the sun, moon, and stars must be moving at very large speeds indeed to go around the earth every 24 hours.

Today, we know that Galileo was right. The earth does rotate, the moon does move steadily around the earth, while the earth and the planets circle the sun at a constant speed. Even the sun moves steadily through our galaxy. But these motions are not along straight lines. The paths swept out by planets are nearly circular. Does this mean that some force prevents them from moving along straight lines? Galileo wondered. Years later Newton supplied an answer!

Sir Isaac Newton—forces and motion

No man did more to untangle the mysteries of motion than Sir Isaac Newton, an Englishman who was born on Christmas day in 1642. Yet, Newton recognized the contributions of Galileo and others when he said, "If I have seen further than [other men], it is by standing on the shoulders of giants."

The brilliance of Newton was evident to scholars in all fields as the famous couplet by the English poet Alexander Pope reveals:

> Nature and Nature's laws lay hid in night:
> God said, Let Newton be! and all was light.

Would you be surprised if a ball suddenly began to bounce? If a book were to slide across a table and fall to the floor? Newton would have been, for he realized that things only start moving when they are pushed or pulled; that is, when a force acts on them. He also noticed that if the force on an object is big enough, the object will *accelerate*.

Dictionaries say that "accelerate" means to "speed up." But to Newton and future scientists, an object "accelerates" when it speeds up, slows down, or *even* when it *changes its direction of motion* with no change in speed.

To find the direction and size of the acceleration when something is changing its speed or its direction, you can easily build one or all of the *accelerometers* in the experiments that follow.

Experiment 9: Testing the bubble or cork accelerometer

Move the bubble or cork accelerometer you have built along a smooth, level surface. As you slowly speed up the accelerometer, notice that the bubble or cork moves in the direction that the speed is increasing. When the accelerometer slows down, the bubble or cork moves in the opposite direction. The bub-

A cork accelerometer: parts (left) and assembled. *Robert Gardner Photo*

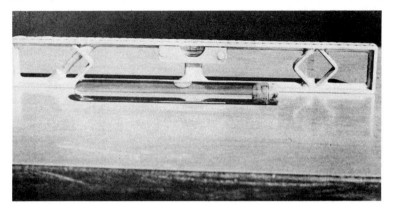

Carpenter's level and a bubble accelerometer. *Robert Gardner Photo*

ble or cork always moves in the direction of the acceleration—the direction that the speed is increasing or decreasing.

Experiment 10: Another accelerometer

Cut a cardboard box as shown in the photograph. Hang a small washer on each side. Draw scales on the cardboard as shown so you can tell how far the weights move during an acceleration. You now have two accelerometers at right angles to each other. It's fun to watch the weights as you travel in a car, but first test the right accelerometer as you did the others to see how the washers move when you accelerate forward (speed up) or backward (slow down) or go around a corner. How is this accelerometer different from the others you built?

Once you have tested the accelerometer to see how it works, tape the box near the window of a car. See if you can predict what will happen to the washers when the car

　　　　　　　　(1) starts moving;
　　　　　　　　(2) speeds up quickly;
　　　　　　　　(3) speeds up slowly;
　　　　　　　　(4) slows down;
　　　　　　　　(5) slows down quickly;

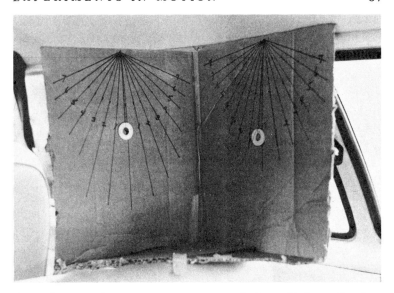

A washer accelerometer near a car window. *Robert Gardner Photo*

> (6) moves at a steady speed;
> (7) goes up or down a hill;
> (8) goes around a corner or curve.

Which washer measures the acceleration when the car changes direction?

Can the car stop faster than it can start?

Can the car accelerate more when it is moving or when it starts from rest?

To see how acceleration depends on force and mass (weight), you can try the next experiment.

Experiment 11: Big pull, little pull

What happens to the acceleration as the force gets bigger? To find out, pull a large toy truck or wagon with a long rubber band. (Or you could pull someone in a wagon and measure the pulls with a spring balance if you have one.)

First, attach the rubber band to the front of the truck. How much do you have to stretch the rubber band to make the vehicle move along with a constant speed? This force is just enough to overcome friction.

Now tape the bubble or cork accelerometer to the truck. Stretch the rubber band so that the force on the vehicle is *more than enough* to overcome friction. Keep the rubber band stretched the same amount as you pull the vehicle. (You may have to practice to keep the rubber band stretched the same amount all along the motion.) Watch the accelerometer. What happens?

To double the force, attach *two* rubber bands to the truck or wagon and stretch both of them the same amount you did one band before. Is the acceleration greater or less than it was with just one rubber band? What happens to the acceleration if you use three rubber bands to pull the truck? How does the acceleration change as the force gets bigger?

Experiment 12: Big mass, small mass

What happens to the acceleration if you increase the mass of the truck (or wagon) by adding stones or weights to it? In this experiment, be sure to use the same force each time you pull a different mass. Why?

Your results will probably be the same as Newton's. He found that when the force on an object was greater than the force of friction, it accelerated. To make the acceleration bigger, he found he had to make the force bigger. If the mass increased, the acceleration got smaller, provided the force remained the same. This isn't very surprising! You know that you can easily accelerate a baseball to a high speed, but it takes a much bigger force to accelerate a bowling ball to the same speed. Cars or trains have so much inertia that very large forces are needed to make them accelerate at all.

But do forces make the planets revolve around the sun? Can there be forces and accelerations if the planets move at nearly constant speeds?

You've seen that an object accelerates in the same direction that the force is pushing or pulling on it. By watching the acceleration of something that is going in circles, you can find out if there is a force, and if there is, you can see in which direction it is acting.

Experiment 13: Round and round

Tape your cork or bubble accelerometer to a turntable or lazy susan. When the table turns at a steady speed, is there an acceleration? Were you surprised? What was the direction of the acceleration? What is the direction of the force that makes something move in a circle?

To find out if the acceleration inward is related to the speed, move the accelerometer closer to, then farther from, the center of the turntable. Where is the speed greatest? Where is the acceleration greatest? Where, on the rotating surface, is the speed zero? Where is the acceleration zero?

See if you can predict the direction of the acceleration when you tape an accelerometer to a playground merry-go-round, a toy train moving on a circular track, a circling bicycle, or a car going around a curve.

Experiment 14: An inward force

When something moves in a circle, the acceleration is inward—toward the center of the circle. The acceleration indicates that there is a force directed inward. Such an inward force is called a *centripetal force*. You can find out how the speed, mass, and radius of a circling object are related to the centripetal force by taping a long, thin rubber band or a chain of smaller rubber bands to a golf ball, a small rubber ball, or a stone. Attach an identical band to a cork or Ping-Pong ball. To see how the force depends on the mass, take the balls outside and swing the heavier ball in a circle. Then swing the lighter ball in a circle at the same rate. How does the ball's mass affect the centripetal force needed to make it move in a circle? You can measure the force by seeing how much the rubber bands stretch.

To see how the centripetal force is related to speed, try swinging one of the balls at different speeds. How does the force change as the speed increases? How can you tell?

From your results in Experiment 13, what happens to the size of the inward force when radius of the circle gets bigger?

To check your results, try another experiment. Pour some water into a pail and swing the pail in a circle that extends from over your head to very nearly the ground.

As you swing the pail faster, do you have to pull harder on the pail? If you add more water to the pail, does the inward force needed to move the pail in a circle increase?

Why do you think the water stays in the pail even when the pail is upside down at the top of the circle?

A boy swinging a pail in a vertical circle. *Robert Gardner Photo*

Sometimes things move along circular paths without any connection to a string, an arm, a turntable, or a rubber band. Where are the centripetal forces that cause the circular motions in these photographs?

This roller-coaster track is banked on the curves. Why? *David Webster Photo*

Why does this hockey player lean inward as he turns? *Robert Gardner Photo*

Why does the skier lean into a turn? *Theodore Tucker Photo*

The man in this "spinning barrel" at an amusement park is "stuck" to the wall. The floor has been removed. Why doesn't he fall? *Robert Gardner Photo*

A centripetal force produces an acceleration inward, but it need not change the circling object's speed; it may only change its direction of motion. This is why Newton defined acceleration as a change in direction as well as a change in speed.

A pair of pulls

A centripetal force is needed to make any object move in a circle. When you swing a pail of water, your arm exerts an inward pull on the pail. At the same time, *you* feel the pail pulling *outward* on your arm. This outward pull is called a *centrifugal force*. Every centripetal force is paired with a centrifugal force, but these paired forces pull on different things. You pull inward *on the pail*. The pail pulls outward *on you.*

From swinging golf and Ping-Pong balls, you know that heavier objects tend to move in bigger circles than lighter ones if both are moving at the same speed. This principle is used to separate solids from liquids or light liquids from heavy ones in a device called a *centrifuge*.

Experiment 15: A bicycle centrifuge

If you mix some fine soil with water in a small bottle, the soil slowly settles to the bottom. The particles of some substances are so tiny that they stay suspended, or "hanging," in a liquid for a long time instead of settling out quickly. To make a suspension, add some fine starch or flour to a test tube or pill bottle of water, cap, and shake. Notice how slowly the particles settle. To speed up the process, you can use your bicycle wheel as a centrifuge. Turn your bike on its side, support it on blocks of some kind, and tape the test tube or pill bottle to the rear wheel as shown in the photograph.

Turn the pedals by hand and make the wheel spin at a high speed. Now, stop the wheel. What has happened to the starch particles?

Repeat the experiment with muddy water. What do you find?

A pill bottle taped to a bicycle wheel. *Robert Gardner Photo*

Try spinning a suspension of cooking oil and soapy water. What happens?

Newton's Push–Push Back Law

When you make something move in a circle by pulling it inward as it moves sideways, it exerts an outward (centrifugal) force on you. Are *all* the forces you exert paired with forces that push or pull on you? If you pull on a door, does the door pull back on you?

Look at the footprint in the photograph on page 76. Notice that the front part of the foot made a deeper impression than the heel.

In order to accelerate forward the walker had to push backward against the earth. Because he was walking on sand his push against the earth is more obvious than it would normally be. How would his footprints change if he were trying to stop after running?

Every time we start moving or stop moving, we have to push

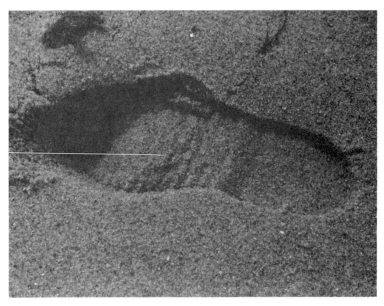

A footprint in the sand. *Robert Gardner Photo*

What makes you think that this truck is starting to move?
Robert Gardner Photo

How does a skater stop? *Robert Gardner Photo*

What evidence do you have from this photograph that a car
changed its speed? *David Webster Photo*

on something. It's the only way we can speed up or slow
down.

Have you ever had trouble controlling a skateboard? If you
have, you know what happens when you *can't* push against
the earth. Perhaps you've tried to walk or have seen cars try
to start or stop on an icy surface. Without friction it's impossible to push against the earth. You can't move forward or stop!

Here's an experiment to convince yourself that you really
do push backward against the earth when you take a step forward.

Experiment 16: Walking on a mini-earth

Find a long, wide board. Place the board on the floor between two sturdy tables so that you'll have something to hang
onto if you start to fall. Next, place some rollers (dowels,
pipes, or round pencils) under the board so that there is very
little friction between the board and the floor. Carefully get
on the board. Be sure the table tops are under your hands so
you can catch yourself if you start to fall. What happens when
you try to walk normally along the board? What happens to
the board? Which way did you push on it?

Take the board off the rollers and place it on the floor. You
can walk along it without difficulty now. Why?

Suppose you can't push against the earth. Is there any way
you can move? There must be! After all, jet planes move

This girl forgot to tie her boat to the dock. She is going to get
wet. Why?

swiftly through the air, and man-made satellites and spaceships maneuver far from earth where there is no air.

Imagine two skaters at the center of a frozen frictionless
pond. How could they get to shore? The experiment below
will help you answer this question.

Experiment 17: Isolated skaters

Ask a friend to help you with this experiment. Both of you
should be on ice or roller skates. Stand behind your friend
and tell him you are going to give him a push. Who moves
when you push him? Or do you both move? Does the same
thing happen if he pushes you? What happens if you push
someone who is much heavier than you? Someone who is
much lighter? What happens if you push on a post or a fence
instead of your friend? Why are you really pushing against the
earth if you do this?

You can do a similar experiment with two toy trucks. Tape
a spring or a spring-type clothespin to the front of one of the
trucks. Then when the trucks are pushed together, they will
push on each other just as you and your friend did. What happens when the spring expands? What happens if one truck is

Toy trucks and spring-type clothespin.

heavier than the other? What happens if the spring pushes against the earth instead of another truck? (To do this, push the truck against a wall to compress the spring.) See if you can predict what will happen if you give the truck with the spring a push so that it collides with another truck. What happens if one truck is much heavier than the other? Does it make any difference whether it is the moving truck or the stationary one that is heavier? What happens if the truck collides with the earth? (A wall will do nicely!)

Now imagine that you are *alone* in the center of a frozen *frictionless* pond. Is there any way you could get to shore? If you remember the spaceship commander's suggestion at the beginning of this chapter, you might throw a wrench if you had one, or you could throw whatever you have in your pockets. An even simpler way would be to blow in a direction opposite to the way you want to go.

To see how blowing air could make you move, try the following experiment.

Experiment 18: A balloon rocket

What happens if you blow up a balloon and then let it go? You can see what happens more clearly if you use a straw to attach the balloon to a string "track" as shown in the picture on page 82.

Which way does the balloon push the air? Which way does the balloon move? How do you know that the expelled air pushed on the balloon?

The next photograph shows a balloon-powered boat made from a cardboard milk carton and a large balloon. If you make the hole in the back of the boat, through which you pull the mouth of the balloon, small enough, the "fuel" in the balloon will last for several seconds. What happens when you let go of the balloon so the air can come out?

You've seen that:

1. A centripetal force is always paired with a centrifugal force.

2. The earth will push on you, if you push on it.

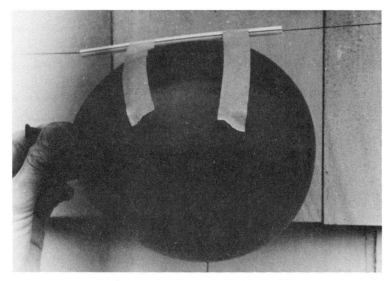

A balloon rocket on a string. *Robert Gardner Photo*

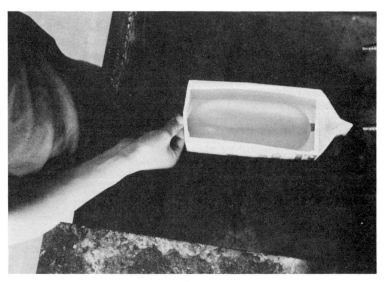

A jet balloon boat. *Robert Gardner Photo*

3. If you push on someone or something, that person or thing automatically pushes back on you.

4. If a "jet" balloon pushes air one way, the air pushes back on the balloon, making it move in the other direction.

Of course, a jet airplane or a spaceship is much bigger than a balloon, but they eject a lot more fuel (hot gases) at a much greater speed. Because they push harder on the fuel they emit, they receive a bigger push in return.

By now you may have drawn the same conclusion that Newton did. He decided that if one object pushes on another, the second object pushes back on the first equally hard but in the opposite direction.

If the two objects pushing against each other are not identical in weight, the less massive (lighter) object will accelerate more than the heavier one; consequently, when the forces stop, the heavier body will not be going as fast as the lighter one. Can you explain why you don't see the earth accelerate to the west when you run toward the east?

Drops and falls

Life on a space station may have its problems, but people living in space don't get bruises from falling down. Down? Down is the direction you fall on earth. No one falls down on a space station because the whole station is "falling" as it orbits the earth. On earth the force that makes us fall is called *gravity*. It's the force that pulls us toward the earth. But don't be fooled! Just because we have a name for it doesn't mean that we know what it is. In fact, no one knows *why* the earth pulls on us. It just does!

There are no strings, springs, or chains binding us to our planet, but one way to think about gravity is to imagine invisible springs holding every object to the earth. If you close your eyes and lift different objects, you can feel these "springs" pulling against you. Heavy objects are connected to sturdy springs; light objects to flimsy weak springs. Does this mean that the acceleration of heavy objects is greater than light ones? To find out, try:

Experiment 19: Falling objects

Drop a heavy ball and a light ball at the same time. Which object falls faster? Or do they fall together? What force makes them accelerate? How do the accelerations of the two objects compare?

Now drop a book and a sheet of paper at the same time. Which one has the greater acceleration? To see if it's the air that slows down the paper place the sheet *on top* of the book. This will prevent air from pushing directly against the paper from below. How do they fall now, when you let go of the book? (If the paper is larger than the book, trim it so it does not extend beyond the book along any edge.)

Another way to reduce air resistance on a falling sheet of paper is to crumple the paper into a ball. Try releasing a crumpled sheet and a flat sheet at the same time. How do their accelerations compare?

If you could eliminate air resistance, how do you think the accelerations of heavy and light objects would compare?

Why do you think skydivers eventually stop accelerating after they reach a maximum speed of about 125 mph?

There is a story that Galileo once dropped two cannon balls, one ten times heavier than the other, from the Leaning Tower of Pisa. It's doubtful that Galileo ever did this dramatic experiment, but he certainly believed that in a vacuum something as light as a feather would fall with the same acceleration as a hammer. Over three hundred years after Galileo's death, astronauts did this very experiment on the airless surface of the moon. By then, no one doubted the outcome, for people had shown that in a long vacuum tube, a feather and a coin fall side by side.

Galileo knew that in a vacuum heavy and light objects fall with the same acceleration. But he wondered how a stone would fall if it were moving sideways when released. He proposed an experiment to find out. He suggested that a sailor drop a stone from the top of a ship's mast. If the ship were not moving, the stone would hit the deck at the base of the mast. But suppose the ship was moving, then the stone would be moving forward when the sailor dropped it. Where would the stone land? You can try a similar experiment to find out.

Experiment 20: Doing Galileo's experiment on a bicycle

Draw a target on a sidewalk or path. Ask a friend, as he rides his bicycle over the target, to drop a stone or a ball at the moment the stone is directly above the target. Where does the stone hit the ground?

Repeat the experiment and watch carefully. Does the stone fall straight down or does it move along with the bicycle as it falls? Where must your friend drop the stone to hit the target?

An even simpler experiment is to drop a bouncy ball as you walk along a hallway. Do you have to stop to catch the ball as

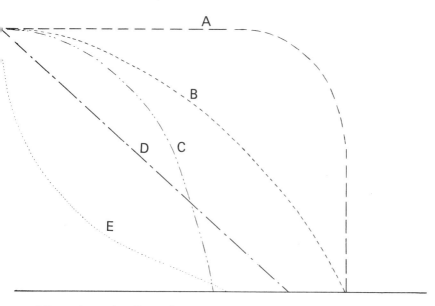

Alternate projectile paths.

it bounces up? Repeat the experiment but this time stop *immediately after* you drop the ball. What happens to the ball?

If you were to drop a ball from the ceiling of a moving train, where would the ball land? If you dropped a stone from the mast of a moving ship, where would it strike the deck?

Using what you have learned in this experiment, which of the paths shown in the drawing on page 85 is like a stream of water flowing horizontally from a garden hose? Which one is most like a cannon ball fired horizontally?

You can follow the path made by water coming from a hose because the stream is continuous. Try it and see! A cannon ball's path is impossible to see. But you can "fire" a marble and see its path. In fact, you can even map its path by doing the next experiment.

Experiment 21: Mapping a projectile's path

Before you can map a projectile's path, you need some way of firing or launching the projectile. You can build a launching pad for a steel ball or marble from a plastic ruler that has a groove down the middle. You will also need a small board, several broad-headed nails, a hammer, and a block of wood. The diagram will help you as you build the launcher.

The paper "rings" shown in the diagram will allow you to map the path of the projectile.

Place the ramp on a table next to a wall or door. Get four or five sheets of heavy paper or light cardboard, each about 5 by 7 inches (12 by 18 centimeters). Fold each rectangle to make a square about 5 inches (12 centimeters) on a side. (The 2-by-5-inch rectangle on the other side of the fold will be used to attach the sheet to the wall.) Cut a circle about 3 inches (8 centimeters) in diameter in the center of the square part of each folded rectangular sheet.

Tape one of the paper ring sheets to the wall about 3 or 4 inches from the end of your launching ramp. Launch a marble or a ball a few times from the top of the ramp. Move the paper ring up or down until the ball or marble goes through

its center. Do the same thing with another ring about 6 to 8
inches (15 to 18 centimeters) from the end of the ramp, a
third ring about 9 or 10 inches (22 to 25 centimeters) from
the end of the ramp, and so on with the remaining rings. As
the path of the projectile becomes steeper, you will have to tilt
the rings for the marble to pass through their centers.

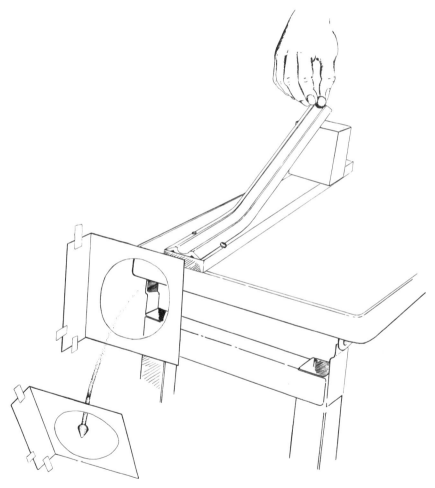

Launching ramp and rings.

How does the path of the ball or marble compare with the path followed by water from a garden hose?

Let the ball roll down the ramp again. At the instant the ball leaves the ramp, drop a second ball to the floor from the same height. You may have to practice a little to release the ball at exactly the right time. When you think you can do it well, listen carefully! Do you hear one thud or two when the balls hit the floor? How do the flight times for the two balls compare?

From the results of your experiments, see if you can answer this question: A bullet is fired horizontally from a gun over a long flat field. At the moment it is fired, a second bullet is dropped from a point beside the gun barrel. How will the time it takes the dropped bullet to fall to the ground compare with the time it takes the fired bullet to strike the ground?

You can test your answer by trying the following experiment.

Experiment 22: Pennies dropped and fired

To do this experiment, you'll need two coins (or washers) and a ruler or thin stick. Place one coin near the edge of a table and the other on the end of the ruler as shown in the drawing on page 90. Use your finger to hold the center of the ruler against the table top. Strike the ruler with your free hand so the ruler suddenly turns toward the coin on the table. It will drive one coin horizontally from the table while the other falls straight to the floor. Listen carefully! Which coin lands first? Or do they hit the floor at the same time?

The photograph shows the results of a similar experiment using two golf balls.

By now you may be able to figure out how Galileo determined the path followed by a cannon ball. He knew that once the ball had been fired, the only force acting on it was gravity; therefore, the ball would fall with the same acceleration as any other falling body. Since there would be no horizontal force on the ball after it left the cannon, it would move hori-

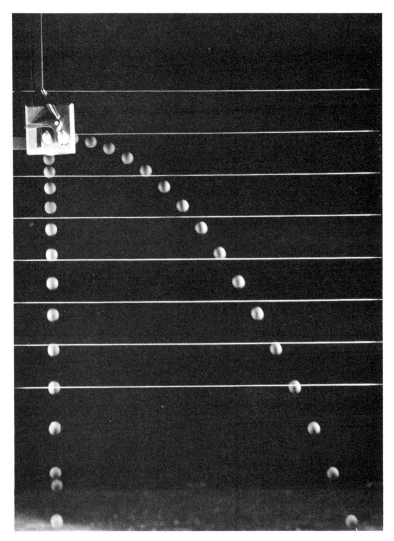

One golf ball was projected horizontally at the same time that the other was dropped. The camera's shutter was held open and a light flashed on every $\frac{1}{30}$ of a second. The white horizontal strings are about 6 inches (15 centimeters) apart. How fast were the balls falling at the bottom of the picture? How can you determine the horizontal speed of the ball that was projected? *Education Development Center, Inc.*

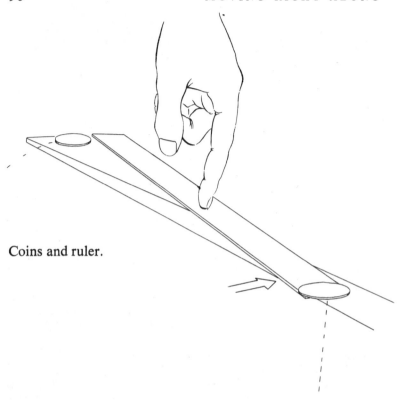

Coins and ruler.

zontally with a constant speed. As you can see from the photograph, the projected ball travels with a constant horizontal speed, but its vertical speed increases in the same way as any other falling object.

Since the flight time of a bullet fired horizontally is the same as a bullet that falls vertically from the gun to the ground, you can actually determine how fast a bullet travels.

Experiment 23: Muzzle velocity

The speed of a shell or bullet as it emerges from a gun is called the *muzzle velocity*. Here's a way to measure the muzzle velocity of a dart gun that fires darts with suction-cup tips (see photo on page 153).

Be sure the gun barrel is level and exactly 4 feet (1.23 meters) above the floor. The room or hallway should be long so that the fired dart will hit the floor and not a wall, a window, or a person. Clear the range! FIRE! Then watch and mark the place where the "bullet" hits the floor. The time it takes to hit the floor is ½ second, since the time it takes an object to fall 4 feet is just ½ second.

Suppose you fire the "bullet" horizontally from a height of 4 feet and it lands 20 feet (6.0 meters) from a point directly below the end of the gun barrel. Since it traveled 20 feet horizontally in ½ second, its muzzle velocity was:

$$\frac{20 \text{ ft}}{0.5 \text{ sec}} = 40 \text{ ft/sec, or } \frac{6 \text{ m}}{0.5 \text{ sec}} = 12 \text{ m/sec}$$

What is the muzzle velocity of the toy gun you used?

Here are the muzzle velocities of some other guns:

Muzzle Velocity

Type of Gun	Feet per second	Meters per second	Miles per hour
.22 rifle	1,100	330	750
Military rifle	2,400	740	1,650
105-mm howitzer	1,550	470	1,050
8-inch howitzer	1,950	600	1,350
Bazooka	275	85	190

What do you predict will happen to the muzzle velocity of your toy gun if you use a heavier bullet? To check your prediction, tape a steel ball or a piece of clay to the end of the dart and repeat this experiment.

See if you can determine the "muzzle velocity" of a baseball that is thrown horizontally.

V

From Pendulums to Planets

What do pendulums, planets, wheels, hi-fi turntables, merry-go-rounds, clocks, and vibrating springs have in common? The answer is that these things move along the same path again and again. A vibrating spring moves back and forth or up and down, a pendulum moves to and fro, the other things move round and round.

To and fro

A pendulum moves back and forth, but you can find a way to change its speed by doing:

Experiment 1: A simple pendulum

Make a pendulum by tying one end of a long string to a washer. Wrap the other end of the string around a pencil taped to the edge of a table, or clamp it between two sticks as shown in the drawing. The washer (or any mass) at the end of the pendulum is called the *pendulum bob*. The length of a pendulum is the distance from its point of support to the center of the bob (the length L in the drawing).

Set the pendulum swinging by pulling the bob an inch or so to one side and releasing it. What happens to the speed of the bob if you make the pendulum longer. If you make it shorter?

The *time* that it takes a pendulum bob to move through one complete swing—over and back—is called the *period* of the pendulum. Adjust your pendulum so that its length (L) is 10 inches (25 centimeters). You will find that its period is 1 sec-

A simple pendulum.

ond. To check up on this, count each complete swing aloud as you watch the second hand of a clock or watch. You will find that it makes thirty complete swings in 30 seconds. How many swings will it make each minute? Each hour?

If you double the length of the pendulum, does its period double? How long must the pendulum be if it is to have a period of 2 seconds? Once you know, see if you can predict how long it should be to have a period of 3 seconds? A period of ½ second?

Does the weight of the bob affect the period? To find out, use *two* washers to make a bob. Measure the period of a 10-inch (25-centimeter) pendulum again. What do you find? What do you think the period will be if you use three washers to make the bob?

Does the distance that the bob swings affect its period? Pull the bob about 2 inches (5 centimeters) to one side, release it, and measure its period. Do it again, but this time pull the bob about 4 inches (10 centimeters) to one side before you release it. Is the period different or the same? How about the speed? Remember,

$$\text{average speed} = \frac{\text{distance}}{\text{time}}$$

See if you can make the bob swing in a small circle or an ellipse instead of to and fro along a line. Does the path that the bob follows affect its period?

From what you have learned in this experiment, see if you can predict the period of a swing in your yard or playground. Just sit on the swing and let it move to and fro; don't "pump"! If a heavier person sat on the same moving swing, would its period change? Would it change if a lighter person were on the swing?

If you sit motionless on a swing, can you make the swing move without touching the ground? As you know from your experiments in Chapter IV, a pull on the swing in one direction should give you a push in the opposite direction. Once you start moving, you probably know how to swing higher by pumping. How does this work? At what point in your swinging motion do you pull on the swing? If you push a young child on a swing, at what point in his motion do you apply a force?

As you've seen, a swing or a pendulum has a natural period, or frequency (swings per second), that depends on its length. By timing your pushes so they occur at the right moment, and at the same frequency as the natural frequency of

Can you figure out how the large pendulum clock in this photograph can be adjusted to run faster or slower? *David Webster Photo*

the swing, you can make the swing move higher. See if you can do the same thing using smaller pushes on a heavy pendulum.

Experiment 2: A push in time

Hang a coffee can filled with water (or some similar heavy object) from a high place such as a beam, a ceiling hook, or a crossbar. Blow through a soda straw so that your breath pushes on this heavy pendulum bob. See if you can time your pushes to make the can swing farther on each swing. Once you have it swinging in a large arc, can you *stop* it by supplying puffs at the right frequency?

Sometimes natural vibrations can create problems! If you cut a piece of tough meat by "sawing" it with your knife and fork, your sawing period may be the same as the natural sloshing frequency of the milk in your glass. What happens then?

Sometimes using the right frequency can solve a problem! The driver of a car stuck in a snow bank can often "rock" the car free by shifting from forward to reverse gears at just the right frequency. A nearly submerged canoe can be at least partially emptied by rocking it at a rate that causes water to slosh over the sides.

Can you think of other examples where natural frequencies are involved in things you do or see?

In a sense, the legs of animals are pendulums with natural periods. Watch a number of different animals as they walk. The period of a giraffe's leg is quite long. It seems to move slowly, but each step covers a large distance. A short-legged dog moves with short quick steps. The many legs of a centipede move with such a high frequency that you can barely follow their motion.

What about people? Watch them as they walk. How does the period of a very tall person's legs (a professional basketball player, for instance) compare with that of the legs of a child?

You can learn a lot by watching and experimenting with a

pendulum, but a pair of pendulums is more than twice as much fun. To see for yourself, try this experiment.

Experiment 3: Coupled pendulums

Tape *two* pencils to the edge of a table top. The pencils should be about 5 inches (12 centimeters) apart. A single

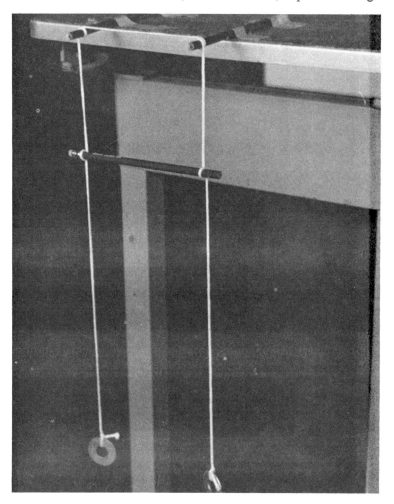

Coupled pendulums. *Robert Gardner Photo*

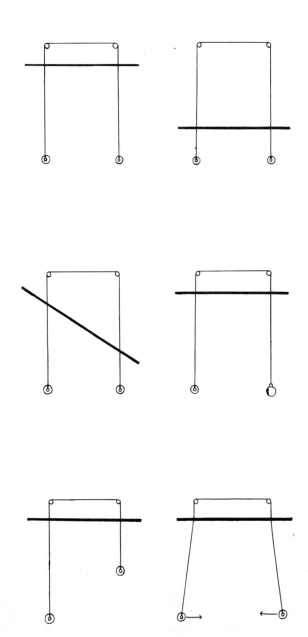

Different types of coupled pendulums.

string about 3¼ feet (1 meter) long can be used to suspend two pendulum bobs. A third pencil is used to connect the pendulum strings as shown in the photograph.

Begin by pulling *one* pendulum bob an inch or so to the side and releasing it. Watch carefully! What happens? Does it affect the other pendulum bob?

Repeat the experiment without the connecting pencil. What do you find? It's fun to watch what happens when you change things in this experiment. The diagrams will give you some ideas! You can probably think of some other things to try.

Up and down

Common pendulums move back and forth, but a "spring pendulum" usually moves up and down.

Experiment 4: A spring pendulum

You can make a "spring pendulum" by attaching a bob to the bottom of a hanging spring. (If you can't find a suitable spring, use a long chain of rubber bands.) Lift the bob a little above its rest position and drop it.

Is the period of your spring pendulum constant or does it change as the distance that the bob falls and rises decreases?

Does the period of your pendulum change if you change the weight of the bob hanging from the spring?

See if you can build a spring pendulum that has a period of 1 second. How heavy is the bob on this pendulum? How much weight do you think you need to make a spring pendulum with a period of two seconds? Try it!

What happens to the period if you double the length of the spring pendulum? You can do this by making a chain of two identical springs. (What can you do if you used a chain of rubber bands?)

What happens if you use a stiffer spring? (You can make a stiffer rubber-band "spring" by using *two* rubber bands rather than one in each "link" of your chain.) Does the period change?

Experiment 5: An undecided spring

Try hanging bobs of many different weights, one at a time, from a spring. Watch the bob as it moves up and down. Be patient! Eventually, you will find a bob that changes the spring's motion from up and down to to and fro (like a common pendulum). Then it will go back to an up-down motion, then to a to-and-fro path, and so on. It can't "decide" which kind of a pendulum it wants to be.

See if you can figure out why this spring pendulum can also behave as though it were a common pendulum.

Round and round

Where can you spend the whole day riding a horse and get nowhere? On a merry-go-round, of course! Anything that goes round and round is another kind of repeating motion. A merry-go-round may not take you anywhere, but your speed depends on where you sit. To see why, try the next experiment.

Experiment 6: Motion on a turntable

Stick three small pieces of opaque tape to the surface of a phonograph turntable. Put one piece on the outside rim, a second at the center, and a third halfway between the other two.

With the turntable rotating, determine the period (the time required to make one complete circle) of each piece of tape. Why are the periods the same? But how do their *speeds* compare? Which piece of tape moves fastest? Which one has a speed of nearly zero? See if you can figure out the speed of each piece of tape!

Where would you sit on a merry-go-round to get the fastest ride? If you've ever played crack-the-whip on skates, you'll know where to ride!

Riding a Ferris wheel or a merry-go-round may be fun, but it's not a very good form of transportation. If you want to go somewhere, you use wheels that roll along the earth as they turn. But how can a wheel that moves around in a circle go anywhere? Does it really move in a circle? To find out, try the following.

Experiment 7: Mapping the motion of a wheel

Tape a marking pen or a crayon to the rim of a tricycle wheel, an old tire, a metal pail, or any disclike object that can be rolled. Have someone hold a long piece of cardboard upright against the tip of the marking pen. As you roll the wheel, the pen will map the motion of the rim on the cardboard. How would you describe the motion of the rim? Is it a circle?

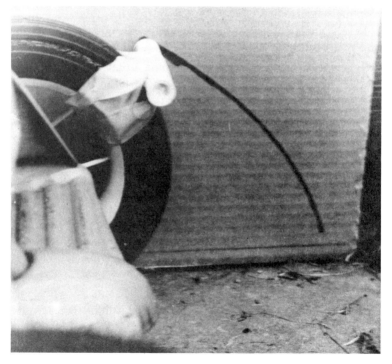

A marking pen mapping the path of a tricycle wheel rim.
Robert Gardner Photo

How can you map the path followed by the center of the wheel as the wheel rolls forward? What kind of a path does it make?

How far forward does a bicycle rider move during each rotation of the wheels? Here's a way to find out!

Experiment 8: Forward around!

Make a mark on the side of a bike tire where it touches the ground. Then draw a line on the ground next to the mark on the tire. Roll the bike forward until the wheel has gone around once. Make a new mark on the ground. The distance between the two lines on the ground is the distance the bike went while the wheel turned around once. How could you determine the speed of a bicycle by knowing the frequency of its rotating wheels?

Ferris wheels, merry-go-rounds, and steering wheels stay in one place as they rotate. They move around an axle fixed to their centers. Can you think of some other wheels of this kind? The wheels on trains, cars, and wagons are also connected to an axle, but they roll as they turn. What happens when a pair of wheels on an axle come to a curve? The wheel on the outside of the curve must go faster than the wheel on the inside because it has farther to go in the same time. To see this for yourself, try the next experiment.

Experiment 9: Rolling wheels

Are the rear wheels of a wagon firmly fixed to the axle? Or can you turn each wheel without turning the other wheel and the axle? Examine a toy wagon and see if you can find out how it is put together.

Pull a toy wagon in a circle. Does the outside wheel go around more often than the inside wheel? Which wheel goes faster? Can you pull the wagon in a circle so that one wheel does not turn at all?

If the wheels were firmly attached to the axle, what would happen if the wagon were pulled in a circle? You can build such a set of wheels and axle from cardboard, a wooden stick, and a pair of thumbtacks. What happens when you try to make this set of wheels move in a circle? How can you change this set of wheels so it will automatically move in a circle when you give it a push?

When an automobile goes around a curve, the wheels on one side have to go faster than those on the other. If you look beneath a car on a lift in a garage, you will find that each front wheel on most cars turns on a separate axle. The rear wheels appear to be connected to the same axle. But look at the bulge in the center of the axle. It contains gears that connect the drive shaft to *two* rear axles. These gears are complicated but they allow the two axles to rotate at different speeds. This arrangement of gears is called the *differential*.

Railroad car wheels are attached firmly to an axle. To allow trains to go around curves, the edge of each wheel is slightly slanted and flanged as shown in the exaggerated drawing. How do such wheels allow the wheels to go around curves even though the wheels are fixed to the axles?

Moving wheels are so common we often forget how important they are. We find them on cars, trains, bikes, planes, even wheelbarrows. We find them in watches, pulleys, pencil sharpeners, gears, and even other wheels. They are very common in machines because they allow us to use small forces to exert

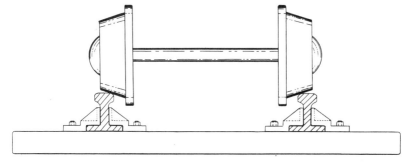

Railroad car wheels.

very large forces. To see how this works, try the next experiment.

Experiment 10: Lifting with a wheel

Turn your bike upside down. Use a string to connect a heavy weight to the inside end of a spoke. By turning the wheel by its tire you can wind the string around the axle and lift the weight.

How does the force you exert on the rim of the wheel compare with the weight of the object you are lifting? If you have a spring balance, you can measure your force on the rim and the force of the weight on the hub. How far does the weight rise when the wheel goes around once?

Do you see now how a pencil sharpener works? A steering wheel? The pedals on your bike? How about the gears on your bike?

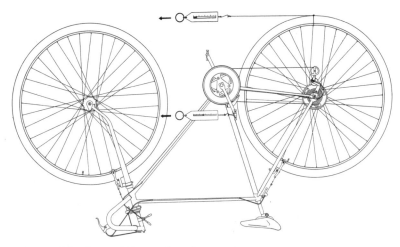

An upside-down bike and spring scales.

Experiment 11: Wheels with teeth

Many bikes are built so that you can change gears. This makes it easier to pedal up hills. You've probably noticed that your bike goes slower when you have it in a gear that makes it easier to pedal.

To find out how gears change your speed and the force you have to exert on the pedals, you will need a bike with two or more speeds and a pair of spring scales. Turn the bike upside down. Use string and tape to tie one spring scale to a pedal and the other to a back tire. The drawing shows you how to connect the scales to the bike.

Start with the bike in low gear—the one you use to go up steep hills. Pull on the pedal with a fairly strong force. At the same time measure the force needed to keep the wheel from turning. Then measure the number of times the wheel goes around when the pedal goes around once. How far would the bike go if the wheel went around once? (Remember Experiment 8!)

Repeat the experiment using a medium and a high gear. Pull on the pedal with the same force you used with low gear. Record your results in a table like the one below so you can remember the numbers.

Gear	Force on pedal	Force on wheel	Number of wheel turns per pedal turn	Distance bike travels forward per one pedal turn
Low	_____	_____	_____	_____
Medium	_____	_____	_____	_____
High	_____	_____	_____	_____

Which gear gives the greatest force to the rear wheel? Which gear makes the bike go farthest for each turn of the pedal?

Wheels were probably first used to make the movement of

heavy objects easier—to reduce the friction involved in dragging them. Let's see how this works.

Experiment 12: Rolling right along

Feel how hard it is to push a heavy book or box along the floor or a table top. (If you have a spring scale you can measure the force.) Then place the books on some round pencils or wooden dowels. How hard do you have to push to move the books now?

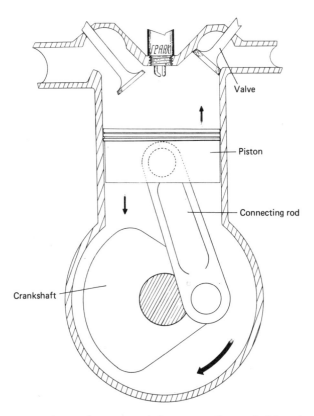

Do you see how the up-and-down motion of this piston is changed to the round-and-round motion of the crankshaft? How is the motion of the crankshaft transferred to the wheels?

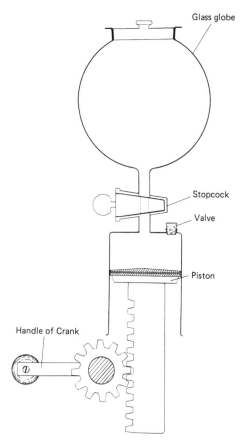

Glass globe

Stopcock

Valve

Piston

Handle of Crank

How is the round-and-round motion of the crank on this ancient vacuum pump changed to the up-and-down motion of the piston?

Up and down, round and round

Sometimes an up-and-down or a to-and-fro motion is changed to a round-and-round motion.

If you watch a round-and-round motion from the side, it looks like a to-and-fro motion. You can see this very easily. Just close one eye and move your index finger in a small horizontal circle with your arm straight out in front of your face. For an even better view, try this experiment.

Experiment 13: Shadows, side by side

Push a pencil into a Styrofoam or clay ball. Use some clay to attach the other end of the pencil near the outside edge of a turntable so that the ball moves in a circle that has a large diameter.

Place the turntable near a light-colored wall. Use a light to cast a sharp shadow of the ball on the wall. How does the shadow move as the ball goes round and round?

The to-and-fro motion of a pendulum coupled with the straight-line motion of a long sheet of paper can be used to make a wave motion. To see how this is done, try Experiment 14.

Experiment 14: A sand pendulum

Punch a hole in the bottom of a small empty can like one that frozen orange juice comes in. Punch two more holes near the top of the can so it can be suspended by two strings as shown in the picture. Fill the can with fine sand and place a wide sheet of paper under it. As you can see, the sand leaves a line marking the path of its swing.

Repeat the experiment but this time pull the sheet of paper beneath the pendulum as it swings. Pull with a slow steady speed. In what direction should you pull so that the sand will make a wave on the paper? Do you see why it makes this pattern?

Experiment 15: Making waves

You can make waves also by giving one end of a Slinky (a coiled-spring toy) a quick to-and-fro motion on the floor while a friend holds the other end firmly in place. To see that it's the wave that moves along the floor and not the Slinky itself, tie a piece of ribbon to one of the coils. How does the ribbon move as the wave moves by it?

Does the speed of the Slinky wave change when it is reflected at the opposite end? How can you find out?

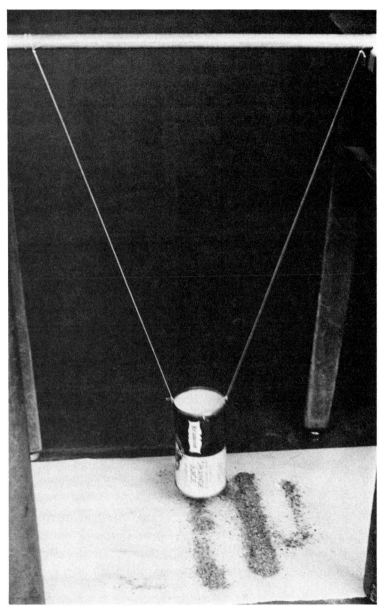

A sand pendulum and paper. *Robert Gardner Photo*

What can you do to make the Slinky wave move faster?

You can also make waves by dipping your finger into a pool of water. To see that it's the wave and not the water that moves away from your finger, place a cork on the water surface. How does the cork move when the waves go by it?

If you watch the cork carefully and make big waves, you will see that it moves in the same way as a swimmer floating on the swells just beyond the breakers at the seaside. He or she moves out toward the approaching wave crest, moves up the front of the crest as he or she is carried toward shore, and finally slides back again down the rear side of the wave into the trough. The swimmer, like the cork (or the molecules in the water if we could see them), moves in a vertical circle as the wave goes by.

When an ocean swell moves into shallow water, the lower part of the wave slows down as it rubs against the earth. The upper part continues at the same speed and so breaks away from its lower portion, spilling its stored energy onto the shore.

Man's biggest merry-go-round

For centuries man has watched the moon wax and wane in its seemingly perpetual motion through the heavens. So regular is its motion that man was able to predict the time of full moon very early in his history. Later he was able to measure the distance to the moon—about 240,000 miles (380,000 kilometers)—a distance so great that he never expected to journey to its surface. But on July 20, 1969, Neil A. Armstrong of the United States became the first man to set foot on the lunar surface. As he stepped onto the moon from the ladder of his spaceship, TV watchers on earth heard him say, "That's one small step for a man, one giant leap for mankind."

Armstrong, together with astronauts Edwin E. Aldrin, Jr., and Michael Collins, had blasted off in Apollo 11 five days earlier from Cape Kennedy. After 2½ minutes the first-stage rocket was cut off and separated. Twelve minutes later the second-stage rocket had carried them into a stable orbit about the earth. They were moving at a speed of nearly 18,000 mph (29,000 kph).

Neil Armstrong, the first man to set foot on the moon, was followed by Edwin "Buzz" Aldrin, shown here stepping from the lunar module ladder. *National Aeronautics and Space Administration Photo*

Two and a half hours later the third-stage rocket was ignited, increasing their speed to 25,000 mph (40,000 kph). At this velocity, they could escape the earth's pull holding them in orbit. They ejected the burned out third-stage rocket and started their long coast to the moon.

By the second day they reached the halfway point. The earth's decreasing but ever present pull had reduced their speed to about 3,000 mph (4,800 kph). By the third day they were only some 38,000 miles (60,000 kilometers) away from the point they planned to enter the moon's orbit. Here the gravitational pull of the moon became equal to that of the earth. Their spaceship, *Columbia,* reached its minimum speed—2,000 mph (3,200 kph). Beyond this point the moon's gravitational pull grew larger and their speed increased to about 4,000 mph (6,500 kph) as they approached the moon on the fourth day of their voyage. A brief firing of the ship's retrorockets slowed the craft to a speed of about 3,700 mph (6,000 kph), placing them in a stable orbit about the moon.

On the fifth day Armstrong and Aldrin entered *Eagle,* the small lunar landing ship attached to *Columbia,* that was to carry them to the moon's surface. After separation from *Columbia,* retrorockets were fired to reduce *Eagle's* speed, sending the ship in a downward arc toward the moon. At 4:18 P.M., Cape Kennedy time, Armstrong piloted *Eagle* to a soft landing on the lunar surface.

After five days of weightlessness, Armstrong and Aldrin could again tell up from down. But the downward pull they felt was only about one sixth as big as the pull they had felt on earth. The 185-pound space suits weighed a mere 30 pounds on the moon. Yet, the 165-pound astronauts retained the same muscle strength they possessed on earth despite the fact that they now weighed only 27 pounds. The weak gravity on the moon enabled them to move easily and swiftly across the moon's dusty surface.

If they had been able to shed their bulky space suits, they

could have set all kinds of records on the moon. A high jump of over 20 feet (6 meters) would have been easy. A major league pitcher who throws a ball horizontally with a speed of 90 mph (145 kph) on earth finds that the ball travels about 80 feet (25 meters) before striking the ground. On the moon the ball would travel about two and a half times as far before hitting the lunar dust. A home-run slugger who can drive a ball 500 feet (150 meters) on earth would be able to hit 3,000-foot (900-meter) homers on the moon. A "tape-measure" homer on earth would go ⅔ mile (1 kilometer) on the moon. Similarly, a good golfer on the earth might drive a ball ⅔ mile from a lunar tee.

There is no air on the moon, so the Apollo 11 astronauts were forced to keep their space suits on in order to breathe and maintain air pressure on their bodies. Still, they were able to move quite well and set up a number of experiments in addition to collecting a number of lunar rock samples to take back to earth.

After the excitement of working on the moon, Armstrong and Aldrin tried to rest before blasting off from the moon aboard *Eagle* on the afternoon of July 21. Following docking with the home ship *Columbia, Eagle* was ejected to remain in orbit about the moon. Rockets were fired for several minutes to get *Columbia*'s speed high enough to escape the moon's gravity and send the spaceship along a path that would bring the astronauts back to earth.

This time *Columbia* lost speed after the rocket firing until it had gone about 38,000 miles (60,000 kilometers). From then on, the earth's pull exceeded the moon's and *Columbia*'s speed gradually increased to 25,000 mph (40,000 kph) before retrorockets were fired to reduce its speed just before it entered the earth's atmosphere, eight days after it had set its sights on the moon.

The story of this trip to the moon is but one of the many involving several spaceships and satellites that have been launched in recent years. Twenty-five years before people would not have believed the speeds at which these vehicles travel. Artificial satellites close to the earth circle the globe once every 90 minutes. This means they travel at speeds of 18,000 mph (29,000 kph) regardless of their size or weight.

Any object dropped near the earth's surface falls about 16 feet (5 meters) during the first second it falls. Because the earth is a sphere, its surface curves away from the horizon by 16 feet (5 meters) every 5 miles (8 kilometers) as shown in the drawing.

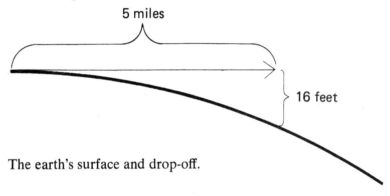

The earth's surface and drop-off.

If a satellite near the earth is to remain in orbit, it must have a speed of at least 5 miles (8 kilometers) per second or it will fall back to earth like any other projectile.

Newton was aware of this as early as the seventeenth century. He pointed out that if a cannon ball could be fired from a mountain top with a speed of 5 miles per second, it would orbit the earth. It was another three hundred years before rockets capable of such speeds allowed us to place satellites in orbit about the earth.

Satellites farther from the earth move more slowly. Communication satellites hover over the same place so that TV and radio waves can be reflected from them. To make this possible, communication satellites must move along an orbit 22,000 miles (35,000 kilometers) above the earth's surface at a set speed. Since they move around their orbit once a day, they travel a distance of 160,000 miles (six and a half times the earth's circumference) every twenty-four hours. What is their speed?

The moon is a satellite of the earth, too, but it is a natural satellite. It circles the earth every twenty-seven days at a distance of about 240,000 miles (380,000 kilometers) from the earth's center. Because it is so far away, it moves with a speed of only 2,300 mph (3,700 kph) relative to the earth (one eighth the speed of man-made satellites close to the earth).

Round and round beyond the moon

We now know that the moon circles the earth roughly every twenty-seven days. But early astronomers believed that the moon went around the earth every twenty-five hours. They thought this because the moon rises about one hour later each day relative to the sun. With a period of twenty-five hours the speed of the moon must be nearly 64,000 mph (100,000 kph).

Similarly, the sun, which they believed circled the earth every day at a distance of 93,000,000 miles, would have had to be moving at the incredible speed of 24,000,000 mph (39,000,000 kph). The planet Saturn which is about 1,000,000,000 miles from earth would have to be moving around the earth even faster—230,000,000 mph.

Early astronomers also thought the stars revolved around the earth, but they didn't know how far away the stars were. Even a star one light-year (the distance light travels in one year) away—and none are as close as that—would have to move with a speed of 1,500,000,000,000 mph in order to go around the earth once a day, which is certainly what the stars appeared to do.

Today, we believe that such speeds are impossible. We believe that objects cannot move faster than the speed of light—186,000 miles per second (300,000 kilometers per second) or 670,000,000 mph. We believe this because scientists who have carefully measured the speed of electrons find that they cannot get even them to go as fast as light no matter how much force they use to accelerate them. (They used electrons because they have very little mass and so can be made to go very fast with very little force.) Since this ultimate speed (the speed of light) cannot be exceeded, we know that the stars cannot go around the earth each day. It must be that the earth turns around every twenty-four hours so that the sun, moon, and stars only *appear* to go around us every day.

But it was other evidence that convinced people that the earth rotates on its axis. In 1851 Jean Foucault, a French physicist, used the motion of a pendulum to prove that the earth rotates.

Foucault knew that a heavy pendulum will keep swinging along the same plane for a long time. If the direction of its swing should appear to change, it would indicate that the earth is turning beneath the pendulum. At the North or South Poles, the pendulum's path would appear to rotate through 360 degrees in twenty-four hours. You can see why this happens by doing Experiment 16.

Experiment 16: A cold pendulum on a turning earth

Build a simple pendulum using a cardboard or wooden box, a string, and a washer. Tape it to a cardboard disc mounted on a turntable as shown in the photograph.

The turntable represents the top surface of the earth. Its center represents the North Pole. Draw a straight line across the disc through the "pole," as shown in the photo. Start the pendulum swinging parallel to the line you have drawn. Slowly rotate the turntable by hand, being careful not to disturb the pendulum's swing. What seems to happen to the direction of the pendulum's swing relative to the earth's "surface"?

What you have seen is what *would have* happened if Foucault had carried out his experiment at the North Pole.

Actually, he did the experiment in Paris, France. From the dome of the Panthéon, he suspended a pendulum 220 feet (67 meters) long. The bob was a 62-pound (28-kilogram) ball of iron. A spikelike structure extended from the bottom

A pendulum on a turntable. *Robert Gardner Photo*

of the ball leaving marks in the sand spread on the floor beneath the bob as it moved to and fro. The period of this pendulum was 16.4 seconds. To be sure it would swing along a
straight line, Foucault released it by burning a string that held
the heavy bob about 10 feet (3.05 meters) from the center of
its swing.

As Foucault had predicted, the path of the pendulum's motion seemed to rotate about 270 degrees in twenty-four hours.
It took about thirty-two hours for the pendulum to turn 360
degrees.

To understand why the pendulum's swing seemed to rotate
less than 360 degrees each day in Paris, you must realize that
the earth is like a huge ball. It rotates about an imaginary center line that goes from the South Pole to the North Pole. The
speed at which any point on the earth's surface is moving
depends on the point's distance from the axis of the earth. If
you lived on the equator, you would move in a circle equal to
the earth's circumference each day. This is a distance of about

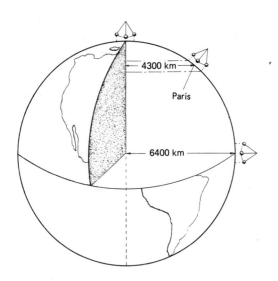

Pendulums at three different places on the earth.

25,000 miles (40,000 kilometers). Your circle would have a radius of 4,000 miles (6,400 kilometers) and your speed would be about 1,000 mph (1,600 kph). If you lived in Paris, you would be about only 2,800 miles (4,300 kilometers) from the earth's axis. You would travel only 17,000 miles (27,000 kilometers) in one day—a speed of about 700 mph. How fast would you travel at the North Pole?

The diagram shows a pendulum swinging along a north-south line in Paris. The point on the earth beneath the southernmost end of the pendulum's swing will move slightly faster than the point below the northern end of the pendulum's motion. The pendulum will appear to rotate relative to the earth. The difference in the earth's speed at the ends of the swing will be such that a 360-degree rotation requires about thirty-two hours. As you can see from the table below, the time for the pendulum to appear to rotate 360 degrees depends on its position on the earth.

° Latitude	Time to turn 360°
90 (North Pole)	24 hr
80	24 hr, 42 min
70	25 hr, 32 min
60	27 hr, 43 min
50	31 hr, 20 min
40	37 hr, 20 min
30	48 hr
20	70 hr, 10 min
10	138 hr, 13 min
0 (equator)	———

At the equator, a point below the southern end of the pendulum will move at the same speed as a point below the northern end of its swing. The pendulum will not appear to rotate at all.

Now that you can prove that it's the earth that turns eastward, not the sun and stars moving westward, see if you can explain why all the stars seem to rotate about Polaris, the North Star!

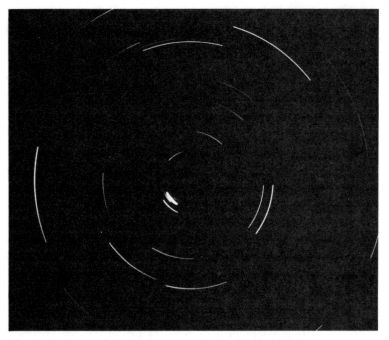

Star tracks about Polaris. *Yerkes Observatory Photograph,
University of Chicago, Williams Bay, Wisconsin*

The Coriolis effect

Because objects near the equator move faster than things
near the poles, strange things happen when air, water,
rockets, and various projectiles move north or south. A rocket
that blasts off from the equator and travels northward is already moving eastward at about 1,000 mph. It keeps this
speed to the east as it moves north, but the eastward speed of
the earth beneath the rocket decreases as it moves farther
northward. The apparent curvature of the rocket path is
called the *Coriolis effect*. The same effect is evident when a
mass of warm air seems to curve eastward as it moves up from
the equator. Can you guess the path that an air mass moving
south from the equator would follow?

The Gulf Stream is an ocean current that flows northward out of the Caribbean. Can you explain why it follows a path that carries it to Northern Europe?

If you wanted to send a rocket from the equator to the North Pole, in what direction would you launch it?

VI

Energy for Motion

Energy is a common word today. Discussions of the energy crisis and sources of energy are favorite topics for TV and radio programs, editorials, and articles in newspapers and magazines.

But what is this energy that everyone talks about? We can't see it! We can't smell or feel it! It's a subtle idea. And a relatively new one at that! The concept of energy arose during the mid-1800s. That may seem like a long time ago to you, but remember, Newton was born and Galileo died in 1642—well over three hundred years ago.

Motion is one of the many forms of energy. You've heard of other kinds too. Heat, light, electricity, and atomic energy are a few. Let's begin by looking at a concept closely related to energy and motion.

Work

To you, work usually means doing something you don't like, such as washing dishes or doing homework, but to a scientist, work has a very different and very definite meaning. It involves two things: (1) a force and (2) the distance that force pushes or pulls something. Work is measured by multiplying the force by the distance through which the force moves:

$$\text{Work} = \text{force} \times \text{distance}$$
$$\text{or}$$
$$W = F \times D$$

If you lift 2 pounds (0.9 kilogram) to a height of 1 foot (0.3 meter), you do twice as much work as you do when you lift 1 pound (0.45 kilogram) through 1 foot. Similarly, you do twice as much work lifting 1 pound through 2.0 feet (0.6 meter) as you do lifting the same weight 1 foot.

Because work involves both force *and* distance, you do no work at all if you push against a brick wall because the wall doesn't move.

If you exert a force of 10 pounds (4.5 kilograms) to push a box 10 feet (3.05 meters) across a floor, you do an amount of work equal to 100 foot-pounds.

Work=10 pounds×10 feet=100 foot-pounds

How does the work you do when you pedal a bicycle compare with the work the bicycle does as it pushes against the earth? You can find out by doing the following experiment.

Experiment 1: Work in, work out

The drawing shows a simple lever. The large black dot near the right end of the lever represents the fulcrum around which the lever may turn. A small force (f) applied to the left end of the lever can exert a large force (F) at the right end of the lever. The large force could be used to lift a heavy weight. Archimedes had such a lever in mind when he said, "Give me a place to stand and I will move the earth."

As you can see from the drawing, the small force moves

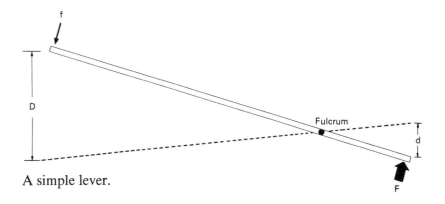

A simple lever.

through a large distance (D) while the big force moves through a much smaller distance (d). With an ideal lever where there is no friction, the work done on the lever will be equal to the work done by the other end of the lever in, say, lifting a weight.

In Chapter V, Experiment 11, you measured the force that the rear wheel of a bicycle exerts when another force is exerted on the pedal. You can easily determine the work done in turning the pedal around once. Just multiply the force on the pedal by the circumference of the circle through which the pedal moves. (The formula for the circumference of the circle is $2\pi r$. That's about 6.3 times the radius of the circle the pedal makes when it goes around.)

You can measure the work done by the rear wheel, too. Just multiply the force it exerts by the distance the wheel moves when the pedal goes around once.

How does the work put into the bike compare with the work the bike does?

The efficiency of any machine is the ratio of the work done by the machine (work out) to the work done on the machine (work in). What is the efficiency of your bike? Is it less or more than one? Why? Does the efficiency of your bike change when you change gears?

Don't be concerned if your bicycle's efficiency is less than 90 per cent. A well-tuned automobile has, at best, an efficiency of 25 per cent. A diesel-powered car may be 35 per cent efficient. The efficiencies of a variety of power sources are shown below:

Power source	Efficiency (in %)
Hydraulic turbine	90
Steam turbine	36
Diesel engine	50
Solar cell	10–25
Steam engine	10
Man	12

Power

If you walk up a flight of stairs, you do some work on yourself. If you run up the stairs, you do the same amount of work but you do it faster. The rate of doing work is called *power*.

$$\text{Power} = \frac{\text{Work}}{\text{time}}$$

Power can be measured in foot-pounds per second, newton-meters per second, or any units of force times distance divided by time. A common unit that you've probably heard of is *horsepower*. One horsepower is 550 foot-pounds of work per second.

James Watt, the Scottish inventor, first used horsepower to measure the rate of doing work in 1783. He simply defined one horsepower as 33,000 foot-pounds per minute, or 550 foot-pounds per second, because he found that a good strong horse could work at about this rate for short periods of time.

To see how much horsepower you can develop, try the next experiment.

Experiment 2: Working like a horse

Have someone measure the time it takes you to run up a flight of stairs. Then measure the vertical distance between the first floor and the second floor. If you know how much you weigh, you can figure out how much power you developed.

$$\text{Power} = \frac{(\text{your weight}) \times (\text{height between floors})}{\text{time}}$$

How much horsepower can you develop?

One of the authors did this experiment. He found that the height from a basement floor to the floor of the second story of his house was 20 feet. He was able to run up the stairs in 6 seconds. Since he weighs 180 pounds, he found his power to be:

$$\text{Power} = \frac{180 \text{ lb} \times 20 \text{ ft}}{6 \text{ sec}} = \frac{600 \text{ ft-lb}}{\text{sec}}, \text{ or } \frac{600}{550} = 1.1 \text{ hp}$$

Ask other people to do this same experiment. You could time them while they run up one or several flights of stairs.

Is the power that people can develop related to their weight? Their height? Age?

Did you find anyone who can truly "work like a horse"? Do you think people could run upstairs for very long?

How could you measure a person's *average* horsepower?

The table below shows the power developed by an average man doing different kinds of work. As you can see, a man can "work like a horse" for only short periods of time:

Kind of work	Period of time	Horsepower developed
Running upstairs	10 sec	0.95
Climbing a treadmill	30 sec	0.65
Mountain climbing (steep)	1 hr	0.20
Mountain climbing (normal)	all day	0.10

Of course, many machines are much more powerful than horses:

Power source	Power developed
Horse	0.6 hp
Volkswagen (Beetle)	48 hp
Piper Cub airplane	65 hp
Lindbergh's "Spirit of St. Louis"	223 hp
Douglass DC-3 airplane	Two 2,400 hp engines
Boeing 747 airliner	Four 164,000 hp jet engines (at 375 mph)
S.S. *Oceanic,* cruise ship	60,000 hp

Energy

When work is done on something, it acquires what we call *energy.* Because that something has energy, it, in turn, is often able to do work on something else.

A pile driver consists of a large weight, or ram, which is lifted and then dropped. The falling weight is used to drive long poles, called *piles,* into the ground. When the ram is lifted, energy is stored in it; therefore, it can do work when it falls.

A pile driver. *David Webster Photo*

You do some work when you wind a watch or a clock. The coiled spring inside the timepiece acquires energy as you tighten it. The spring is then able to do work on the gears inside. The gears, in turn, do work on the hour, minute, and second hands, making them move.

A watch spring is an example of *potential energy*. Energy is stored in the spring so that it has the potential to do work. The same is true of the stretched rubber band in a slingshot, the compressed air in a BB gun, an elevated pile driver, the chemicals in a flashlight battery, even the chemicals in the food we eat.

If we push an object through a distance, we do work on that object and it moves. The speed it acquires depends on how much work we do on it. The energy associated with its motion is called *kinetic energy*. When water flows over a dam, gravity works on the water giving it more and more kinetic energy. Can you think of other examples where gravity does work?

The kinetic energy (*KE*) of a moving object is equal to one half its mass (*m*) multiplied by its speed (*v*) squared:

$$\text{Kinetic energy} = \tfrac{1}{2} \text{ mass} \times \text{speed} \times \text{speed},$$
or

$$KE = \tfrac{1}{2} mv^2$$

A car moving at a speed of 60 mph (96 kph) has four times as much kinetic energy as one traveling 30 mph (48 kph). Do you see why? Remember—to find the kinetic energy you have to square the speed!

The faster car can do four times as much work as the slower car if it collides with something. Similarly, stopping the faster car will require four times as much work as stopping the slower one. If the drivers of both cars lock their brakes, the friction of the road on the tires will do work on the cars and stop them. But the faster car will skid four times as far as the slower one. These are the reasons why speeding is so dangerous!

Conservation of energy

To make a pendulum swing you do some work on it. By raising the bob a small height as you pull it to the side, you give it some potential energy. When you release it, it swings downward, gaining kinetic energy as gravity works on it. Beyond the mid-point of its swing, the bob loses speed but acquires potential energy again. How does the potential energy it gains at the end of its swing compare with the potential energy that you gave it?

From the experiments you did in Chapter V, you know that the pendulum swings to very nearly the height from which you released it. It regains almost all its potential energy. Of course, the pendulum eventually stops. The energy seems to disappear. What happens to the energy? Careful examination shows that the missing energy can be accounted for by a very slight increase in the temperature of the string and surrounding air. This heat was created by friction on the string or collisions of air molecules with the bob. This increased kinetic energy of molecules is known as *thermal energy,* or, more commonly, *heat.*

Energy may be transferred or transformed from one kind to another, but experiments show that it is never lost. Energy is never created or destroyed—it is always conserved.

Energy to energy

Energy is changing from one form to another constantly. The potential energy stored in the weights of a pendulum clock is converted to the kinetic energy of the gears and the swinging bob. The chemical energy in the food you eat is transformed into kinetic energy when you run or into gravitational potential energy when you pedal your bike up a hill. Gravity can do work on you and your bike as you gain kinetic energy coasting down hill. The potential energy of water is changed to kinetic energy as the water flows down a river. If a dam crosses the river, the kinetic energy of the water falling over the dam may be used to turn a turbine connected to a generator and produce electrical energy.

In all these energy transfers, some heat is produced. Friction within your body, between your bike and the road, and between flowing water and the earth, the dam, and the turbine all produce some heat. It is for this reason that inventors who tried to produce perpetual-motion machines never succeeded. And they never will! We know now that such a machine is impossible. Whenever energy is transferred, a little of the energy rubs off as heat. If we convert potential energy to work, we never get as much work out as we put in; a little heat is always produced in the process.

One inventor who thought he could make a simple perpetual-motion machine built one that you can copy by trying Experiment 3.

Experiment 3: Perpetual motion

Look at the simple machine at the left in the photograph. The inventor thought that capillary action (the rise of liquids up thin tubes) would keep water flowing up and out of the curved tube. You can build a series of such tubes using a paper towel like the one on the right side of the photograph. A paper towel consists of many wood fibers pressed closely together. Water will move up through the narrow spaces between these fibers if the towel is dipped into the liquid. (It is this behavior that paper-towel manufacturers advertise to sell their products.) A little food coloring in the water will help you to see the movement of the liquid a bit more clearly.

Elastic potential energy

Energy stored in springs keeps watches ticking. This kind of energy is appropriately called *elastic potential energy*. The spring pendulum that you built in Experiment 4, Chapter V, was an example of elastic potential energy. When you lifted

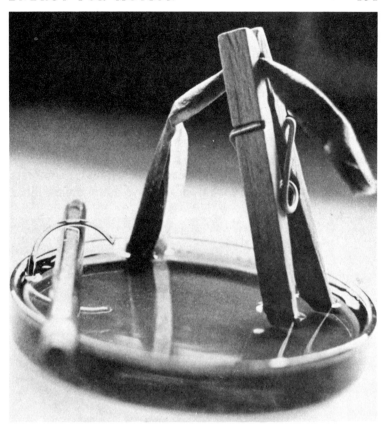

A tube and a paper towel. Does this perpetual-motion machine work? Try it and see. *Robert Gardner Photo*

the weight to start the pendulum, you gave it some gravitational potential energy. As the weight fell, it lost its potential energy and gained kinetic energy, while transferring elastic potential energy to the spring. At the bottom of its motion, the weight stopped for a moment. Practically all its original gravitational potential energy had been changed to elastic potential energy in the spring. As the spring contracted, the mass rose. The elastic potential energy stored in the spring was converted back to the gravitational potential energy of the raised weight. Of course, here, as everywhere, the motion will eventually stop. The only evidence of the original work done is a very slight rise in the temperature of the air surrounding the spring. Careful study will show that the total heat produced is equal to the work done in lifting the weight to start the motion.

Electrical energy

Electric motors can lift weights, pump liquids, compress gases, and even provide the power to move automobiles. Since

Where is the elastic potential energy here? What other forms of energy will be seen when the elastic potential energy disappears? *David Webster Photo*

electricity can be used to do all this work, it, too, is a form of energy.

You've seen that the force of gravity can be used to do work. To see several examples of electrical forces doing work try Experiment 4.

Experiment 4: Electricity at work

In the winter, when the humidity in your home is low, you can create an electric force by rubbing a plastic ruler, pen, or comb with some woolen clothing. Bring the plastic object that

A water stream bent by an electric charge. What evidence do you have that electrical forces are doing work on the water? *Robert Gardner Photo*

is now electrically charged near some tiny pieces of paper. Were you able to do some work on the paper?

Recharge the plastic object and bring it near a narrow stream of water flowing from a tap as shown in the photograph on page 133.

The round-and-round motion of a turntable, an electric mixer, or a power drill; the back-and-forth motion of a sander or an electric knife; the up-and-down motion of an elevator or a saber saw—all these motions are powered by the energy from electric motors. To build a simple electric motor try the following experiment.

Experiment 5: An electric motor

To build a simple electric motor, you will need a magnetic compass, a flashlight battery, and a piece of insulated wire.

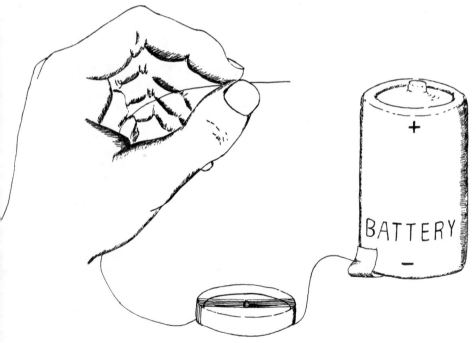

A D-cell battery, compass, and wire.

Wind the insulated wire around the compass so that it is parallel with the compass needle as shown in the drawing.

Leave several inches of wire at each end of the wire coil so that you can connect the coil to the battery. (You will have to sandpaper or strip the insulation from the ends of the wire to make good electrical contact between the battery and the wire.)

Tape one end of the wire to one pole of the battery. Briefly touch the other pole of the battery with the other end of the wire. What happens to the compass needle when electricity flows through the coil? By touching the wire to the battery and then removing it at just the right time you can get the compass needle to turn round and round. How could you use this simple motor to do work?

What is the source of the electrical energy that turns motors, lights bulbs, heats stoves, and powers radios and TV sets? When you rubbed a plastic object with wool, you created

One of the giant turbines in an electric power plant. *Courtesy of Canal Electric Company. Photo by Samuels Studio Inc.*

an electric force that enabled you to lift paper or bend a water stream. When you used a battery to turn the simple electric motor made from a compass, the chemicals in the battery supplied the energy. When you turn on an electric mixer, a power drill, or an electric light, the electric energy comes from a power plant. In the power plant, giant generators consisting of huge wire coils turning in magnetic fields produce the electricity. The coils are connected to turbines which can be turned in a number of ways. Some are rotated by the conversion of the potential energy at the top of a dam to the kinetic energy of the falling water. The water falls on the turbine blades causing them to turn. In many other power plants the turbines are driven by jets of steam. The steam is produced by heating water with burning oil or coal. An increasingly common source of the heat used to generate steam comes from atomic reactors. The nuclear reaction does not itself create electricity—it only produces heat which is used to make the steam needed to turn the turbines.

Chemical energy

When coal, oil, and wood are burned, heat is produced. Some of this heat energy can be used to increase the kinetic energy of water molecules. As the water molecules move faster and faster, they eventually fly apart and the liquid becomes a gas that we call steam. The heat released when wood, coal, or oil burn was stored in the chemicals that make up these substances. This form of stored energy is still another kind of potential energy that we call *chemical energy*. It is the same form of energy that is stored in the food we eat. Our bodies "burn" food slowly, producing the heat we need to stay warm, as well as the energy we need to carry on an active kinetic-energy-filled life.

But what is the source of the potential energy stored in food, wood, and fossil fuels?

Light energy

You can tell that light is a form of energy because it can be changed to heat just as other kinds of energy are. But unlike other sources of energy, light comes to us free of charge from the sun.

Under the right conditions light can be converted to chemical energy as well as to heat. This means that light energy can be stored as a form of potential energy. But how?

The green plants that cover much of the earth's surface (in the oceans as well as on land) are able to "capture" light and store it as chemical energy in the food they manufacture. The process by which plants trap light energy and store it in food is called *photosynthesis*. During this process the green plants use the energy in sunlight to convert carbon dioxide and water into food and oxygen. Since the food contains more energy than the carbon dioxide and water from which it was made and since photosynthesis cannot take place in the dark, light must be the source of this extra energy.

The oxygen produced during photosynthesis is the same gas we breathe, the gas that most living things need to carry on respiration.

Since only green plants are capable of carrying on this magnificent process, the earth's entire source of food and oxygen comes from these plants. Without them, life on this earth would be impossible.

The chemical energy in the coal and oil we use to produce heat and electrical energy came from sunlight too. But the conversion of light energy to the chemical energy stored in these fuels took place many eons ago. Coal and oil are the decomposed remains of plants that grew on earth millions of years before man appeared on this planet.

Of course, plants are still being decomposed, but the conversion of dead plants to coal and oil takes a very long time. During the last hundred years we have used a large fraction of the coal and oil that was made over the last billion years. Because man's use of energy has grown so rapidly recently, we anticipate that we may exhaust the world's available oil supply in fifty years and its coal in another century or two. In addition, burning coal and oil pollutes the atmosphere, so we really face two kinds of energy crises:

1. Our major energy sources are running out.
2. The use of our present energy sources adds undesirable substances to our atmosphere, our soil, and our water.

We need not only new sources of energy but sources that will not pollute the environment.

New sources of energy: atomic and solar

When coal burns, atoms of carbon combine with atoms of oxygen to form molecules of carbon dioxide gas. Because heat is released during this process, we know that there is less chemical energy in carbon dioxide than there was in the carbon and oxygen before they combined. The loss of potential energy that appears as heat during the burning of coal might well be called *atomic energy* since it comes from the energy stored in atoms. However, the words *atomic energy,* as they are commonly used, refer to a much more potent source of energy, the energy released during the fission or fusion of atoms themselves.

The atoms of any element consist of two parts. There is a tiny, dense, positively charged core called the *nucleus.* The nucleus contains protons and neutrons and constitutes practically all the atom's mass. Protons and neutrons have just about the same mass, but neutrons carry no charge while protons each carry 1 unit of positive charge. The second part of the atom is made up of electrons, which move about the nucleus at distances one thousand times or more the diameter of the nucleus. An electron has only one two-thousandth the mass of a proton, but each carries one unit of negative charge. Since an atom has equal numbers of protons and electrons, that is, the same number of positive and negative charges, its over-all charge is zero.

All uranium atoms have ninety-two protons in their nuclei, but some uranium nuclei have different numbers of neutrons than others. These different kinds of uranium atoms are called isotopes. (Many other elements share this property of having atomic nuclei with different numbers of neutrons. Under the right conditions, uranium nuclei with 143 neutrons (uranium 235) will split to form lighter nuclei. During this process, called *fission,* several neutrons are released. These escaping neutrons can collide with other uranium nuclei with 143 neutrons and cause *them* to fission. If enough uranium nuclei are present, the neutrons released by one uranium nucleus can split two more nuclei in other uranium atoms, the neutrons from these two can split four other nuclei, the neutrons from these four can split eight nuclei, and so on. Once this chain reaction starts, it takes but a fraction of a second before a huge number of uranium atoms will have undergone fission.

The smaller nuclei of such atoms as barium and krypton that are produced when a uranium atom splits have less total mass than the original uranium nucleus. The missing mass is transformed into energy. The amount of energy released is equal to the missing mass multiplied by the speed of light squared. This can be summarized by the now famous equation: $E=mc^2$. Because the speed of light is so large—186,000 miles (300,000 kilometers) per second—a small decrease in mass releases an enormous quantity of energy.

In the explosion of an atomic bomb, a very large number of uranium nuclei are fissioned, releasing vast amounts of energy in an instant. Such explosions are extremely destructive and hardly the solution to our energy crisis. However, it is possible to control a fission reaction. Once a fission reaction starts the rate of fission can be controlled by surrounding the small rods of uranium 235 with graphite and using boron steel rods to absorb neutrons. In this way, energy can be released slowly enough to heat water to steam. The steam can then be used to turn turbines in the same way that it is done in coal- or oil-burning power plants.

A number of these atomic power plants have already been built in various places throughout the world. You will generally find them near large bodies of water because water is needed to carry away the large quantities of heat produced by atomic reactions.

While atomic power plants now produce some of our electrical energy, many people do not believe that nuclear fission is the solution to our energy crisis. Atomic power plants are very expensive to build and there is always the possibility of an accident that might release dangerous radioactive materials into the environment. There is also the problem of

An atomic power plant at Plymouth, Massachusetts. *Boston Edison Company Photo*

disposing the radioactive wastes that accumulate in the plants during the fissioning of the uranium. These wastes are now buried in desolate areas, frequently in deep salt mines. But it takes thousands of years for them to disintegrate into safe substances. Further, the wastes have to be transported from the power plant to the burial area. An accident along the way might release radioactive materials.

Controlled nuclear fission may meet some of our future energy needs, but there are clearly dangers in such a solution.

The process associated with a hydrogen-bomb explosion is an even more potent source of energy than uranium fission. To detonate a hydrogen bomb a very high temperature is required—such as that produced by the fission of uranium; in fact, the detonator for a hydrogen bomb *is* a fission bomb. When a hydrogen bomb goes off, it is again a loss of mass that accounts for the enormous amount of energy released. However, the decrease in mass occurs during a process that is called *fusion*. During fusion, nuclei of hydrogen fuse (join) to form nuclei of helium. The helium nuclei formed have slightly less mass than the total mass of the hydrogen nuclei combined to form them; the missing mass is transformed into energy.

If scientists and engineers can figure out a way, using lasers or some other technique, to produce the high temperatures needed to set off a fusion reaction whose rate of energy released can be controlled, fusion might well solve our energy crisis for ages. There is certainly an abundance of the hydrogen isotopes used in fusion in the waters of our oceans. But the problems involved in igniting and controlling fusion are difficult and numerous. The earliest date forecast for controlled fusion power is probably at least twenty-five years away.

Of course, we have a gigantic source of fusion power only 93,000,000 miles away—our sun. There, over 650,000,000 tons of hydrogen are converted to helium every second. The resulting helium is several tons less massive than the hydrogen from which it comes, and the missing mass appears as the energy emitted by the sun.

The sun is in fact undergoing a continuous hydrogen-bomb explosion of fantastic size and intensity. Some of the resulting energy falls on our earth in the forms of light and heat. It is our only outside source of energy and it's free. We don't have to mine it, drill it, or refine it. We can't use it to make food the way green plants can, but it does keep our planet warm, makes our weather, and, through the work of green plants, ultimately provides us with the food we need to live.

Because sunlight is free, nonpolluting, and, in many places, plentiful, it may be the solution to our energy crisis in some parts of the world. Buildings with solar heaters on their roofs are becoming more common in America. By using the sun's energy to heat buildings and the water we use for baths, showers, and washing clothes and dishes, we can reduce our need for energy from coal, oil, and electricity.

You can build a simple solar heater yourself by doing the following experiment.

Experiment 6: A solar heater

Find two cardboard boxes, one slightly larger than the other. The smaller box should fit into the larger one with some space between them. Fold the flaps on the open side of each box into the box itself. Paint the inside surface of the smaller box with flat black paint or line it with black paper. Tape a thermometer to the bottom of the box and cover the open side with clear plastic wrap. Tape the edges of the plastic wrap to the sides of the box so that the plastic is tight across the top and air cannot enter or leave the box. Place this smaller box inside the larger one. Then tape another piece of plastic wrap over the open top of the larger box.

Place your solar heater in a sunny place. Tilt the box so the sunlight falls directly on the "double window." Place a second thermometer outside the box in the sunlight. Compare the temperatures inside and outside the box. What do you find?

If air could be circulated through a larger heater of this kind it could be used to warm the air in a room. If coils of

Solar panels on a house. *Solarex Corporation Photo*

tubing were laid along the bottom of such a heater, water could be heated and circulated through a building.

Solar heaters will reduce heating and electric bills, but the direct conversion of light to electricity would be an ideal solution to the energy crisis.

Many man-made satellites are powered by solar cells that convert light to electrical energy. Unfortunately, the cost of generating electricity on earth with solar cells is many times greater than present methods that use coal or oil. Such cells are expensive to make and produce very little power, and a large number of cells must be used to produce a significant amount of electricity. A communications satellite, for instance, may require 20,000 solar cells to produce the power it needs.

Scientists hope to find materials that will convert light to electricity more efficiently than the ones in use today. Research has already improved the efficiency of solar cells from 5 per cent to nearly 25 per cent. As better materials are devel-

The electricity that makes this little motor turn is obtained from sunlight. The solar cell connected to the motor converts sunlight to electricity. *Robert Gardner Photo*

oped and the cost of manufacturing them is reduced, the conversion of light to electricity may be a solution to the energy crisis, for some areas of the world at least.

Some scientists believe that it may be possible to place solar-cell power plants in orbit above the earth. Such satellites would not have to contend with clouds and the atmosphere that drastically reduce the solar energy reaching the earth's surface. These satellites could convert the light to beams of microwaves. The microwaves could be transmitted to stations on earth where the energy could be converted to electricity. Whether such satellites can ever produce electricity economically is a question that only extensive research can answer.

The electricity that powers the appliances in our homes and industries, as well as the energy that moves our cars, planes, and trains, comes from coal and oil today. These energy sources are being used up rapidly. Will we replace these sources of energy for motion in our modern world with the energy from nuclear fission, nuclear fusion, or sunlight? Probably all of these, and some others will play a part. During your lifetime the major energy source used to generate motion will change. No one knows which sources of energy will best serve mankind in the future. What do you think will happen?

1,

2

9.

~10

12!

Motion Puzzlers

1. This time-lapse photograph shows part of the circular path of stars around the north star. But what do you think caused the bright line across the star trails?

Table Mountain Observatory Jet Propulsion Laboratory, Wrightwood, California, Photo

2. Why does a cyclist lean inward when he goes around a curve? Can you ride your bike around a corner without leaning?

3. When you go around a corner in a car you are "thrown" against the outside of the curve the car is turning. Why aren't astronauts thrown against the outside of the curve of their spaceship as they circle the earth?

4. On roads or driveways covered with gravel, the gravel gradually builds up on the outside edge of the curves in the road. Why?

5. Suppose you put some whole milk in a centrifuge and spun it. When you removed the milk from the centrifuge, which would be on top, the milk or the cream?

6. A candle is burning inside a glass chimney that is moving in a circle on the outer edge of a turntable. Will the candle flame point inward, outward, or upward as it normally does?

7. This photo shows some children running down a sand dune. How can you tell whose arms and legs were moving fastest?

David Webster Photo

8. Place a cardboard disc on a phonograph turntable. When the turntable is revolving, you can easily draw a circle on the disc. How do you do this? But can you draw a straight line from the center to the edge of the disc while it is spinning? Try it!

9. If a steel ball was dropped from a very high tower, would it land east or west of the point directly below its release position?

10. Look at the vapor trail left by an airplane as shown in this photograph. Which way was the plane moving?

Robert Gardner Photo

11. When man-made satellites are sent into space, they usually are launched from west to east at points near the equator. Why is this done?

12. You are standing on a bridge over a highway. As a car passes below you someone throws a baseball sideways out of the car's window. Which of the paths below best describes the path the ball will follow as seen by you?

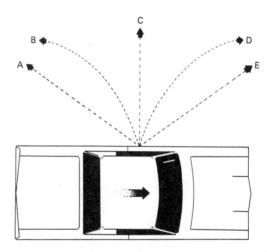

Alternate paths of a baseball thrown from the window of a moving car.

13. Why do Mexican jumping beans jump?

14. Place a toy car or truck on a wide board. Lock the front wheels with a rubber band or by wedging a piece of paper between the wheels and the body. Raise the board until the car begins to move. Repeat the experiment with the back wheels locked and the front wheels free to roll. In which case does the car go into a spin as it moves?

15. The front brakes on most cars are bigger and stronger than the rear ones. Why?

16. When a driver steps on the brake pedal, why are the front brakes made to grab before the rear ones?

inertia

17. A man, a horse, and a car are lined up for a 30-foot race. Who will win?

18. If you drive through a drizzle in a car, the raindrops appear to be falling at an angle. Yet when the car stops, the drops are seen to be falling straight down. Why is this?

19. Imagine yourself getting on an elevator on a high floor in a tall building and standing on a bathroom scale. Suddenly the elevator begins to move downward. Will your weight, as measured on the scale, appear to increase, decrease, or remain the same? What will happen when the elevator slows down?

20. A large hot-air balloon with a basket suspended below it is seen moving along at an altitude of several hundred yards. Do the passengers in the balloon feel any wind?

21. You are standing on the platform of a railroad station when a train passes by at 60 mph (100 kph). A man standing on the rear platform of the train throws a baseball in a direction opposite to the direction the train is moving. He throws the ball with a speed of 60 mph at the moment the train passes in front of you. Where will the ball strike the tracks? What path will you see it follow?

22. A train is moving forward. What points on the train are moving backwards?

23. Why do wagon wheels seen in movies sometimes appear to be motionless or even moving backwards when the wagon is moving forward?

24. England and Western Europe are considerably warmer than Newfoundland, which is located at the same latitude. Can you explain why?

25. When you walk, you push against the earth. The earth pushes back causing you to move forward. But a spaceship has no earth nor even air to push against. If it was to stop in space, how could it ever start moving again?

26. How does a skater get started on smooth ice? Once started, how does a skater manage to speed up or slow down?

27. When a tall smokestack falls, it always breaks in the way shown in the photograph. Why does it break this way?

The (*Louisville, Ky.*) Courier-Journal. *Reprinted with Permission*

28. Which of the two "bullets" will land first if the gun in the photo is "fired" horizontally over a level floor?

Robert Gardner Photo

29. Is it easier to push or pull a wheelbarrow?

30. Why won't these perpetual-motion machines work?

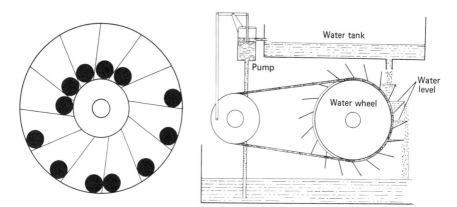

"Perpetual-motion" machines.

31. Why is it easier to unroll a full roll of toilet paper than one that is nearly empty?

32. (a) Place a yardstick or a meter stick on your two index fingers. Your fingers should be near opposite ends of the stick. Slowly move your fingers together. Where do they meet on the bottom of the stick?

(b) Repeat the experiment, but this time start with one finger near the middle of the stick. Where do your fingers meet this time?

(c) Repeat the experiment again. Before you start, place a lump of clay on top of the stick near one end. Where do your fingers meet this time?

How do you explain the results of these experiments?

33. What motion is seen in this photograph?

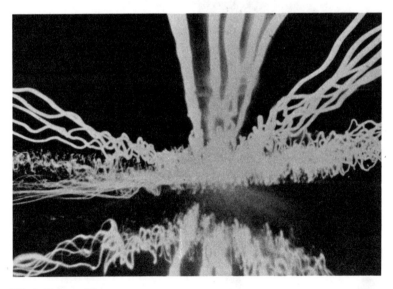

Nick Foster Photo

Answers to Motion Puzzlers

1. A shooting star crossed the star paths while the camera shutter was open. (See page 120.)

2. An inward (centripetal) force is needed to make an object move in a circle. By leaning inward the cyclist causes the wheels of the bike to push outward against the road or path. The road pushes back with an equal force, supplying the centripetal force needed to make the bike follow a circular path. (See page 69.)

3. When a car goes around a curve, the passengers tend to continue along a straight line. Since the car is turning, the people eventually bump against the side of the car. The car then supplies the centripetal force that makes the passengers move along the arc of a circle with the car. In a spaceship orbiting the earth, the inward force is supplied by gravity. It gives the ship and the astronauts the same centripetal acceleration. Therefore, the ship and its occupants "fall" together, producing a sensation for the astronauts that we call "weightlessness." (See pages 62, 69.)

4. To go around curves, cars must get an inward (centripetal) force. They obtain this force by the outward push of the tires against the road. This outward force pushes any loose gravel to the outside of the turn.

5. The cream will be on top. It is "lighter" than the skim milk below it. (See page 74.)

6. The candle flame consists of gases that are lighter than the air around them. The flame will behave like a cork or bubble accelerometer. It will point inward. (See pages 65, 66, 69.)

7. The relative speeds can be determined by the degree of blurring in the photograph.

8. To draw a circle simply hold the point of a pencil on the cardboard. The spinning disc will draw the circle for you. A radial line is hard to draw. You must move your pencil outward and in the direction that the disc is turning at the same time. The task is made even harder by the fact that the speed of the disc increases as you move outward.

9. Slightly east of the tower. The path traveled by an object on earth is circular when seen from afar. As we get farther from the center of a rotating circle we move faster. A person on the outside of a merry-go-round moves much faster than someone near the center. The ball at the top of the tower will be moving faster than the earth at the base of the tower so it will travel a tiny bit farther eastward during its fall than the point directly beneath it. (See page 100.)

10. Downward in the photograph. Vapor trails tend to spread with time. Apparently this plane moved across an air current.

11. The earth turns from west to east. It moves fastest at the equator where the surface is farther from the earth's center. Satellites already possess this speed at their launching sites.

12. You will see the ball move both sideways and forward: Path E.

13. Mexican jumping beans are the seed pods of the arrow plant. A certain moth lays its eggs on the seed pods. When the eggs hatch, the larvae (worms) bore into the pods and feed on the seed material inside. When the seed pods fall off the plants, the larvae are still inside. In response to the sun's heat, the larvae inside the pods grasp the silk that it has attached to the pod wall. They then snap their bodies against the wall of the pods, causing them to move. In this way the larvae keep turning different sides toward the sun until the pods land in a shady place. Mexican boys collect these "beans" and sell them to dealers who sell them to novelty stores. The beans stop jumping after several months because the larvae enter the pupal, or resting stage, in their life cycle.

14. The car will spin around when the back wheels are locked.

15. Normally there is more weight on the front wheels than the rear ones. The extra weight on the front wheels increases the friction between the tires and the road. When the car's brakes are applied, inertia causes the car's body to tip forward putting still more weight on the front wheels. This increases the friction and tends to keep the tires from sliding. (See page 63.)

16. So the rear wheels will continue to roll and maintain friction with the road. Try the experiment suggested in Puzzler 14.

17. The man will win. The car and horse have too much inertia to accelerate very fast. Of course, a car will win a long race because it can go much faster, given time to accelerate to its maximum speed. (See page 68.)

18. The drops appear to fall at an angle because the car is moving toward the drops as they fall straight down.

19. As the elevator starts down, your weight appears to decrease. The scales fall away from you as the elevator accelerates downward. As the elevator begins to slow down your weight will appear to increase. What would happen to your apparent weight if the elevator accelerated upward from rest?

20. No! They are moving with the wind.

21. You will see the ball fall at your feet. It will fall straight down to the track.

22. The bottom of the flanges on the wheel extend below the top of the track. The point of the wheel in contact with the track has a speed of zero. Points below that will be moving backward. (See page 101.)

23. If the movie camera takes a picture every time the wheel

rotates once, the wheel will appear to be stationary. Or if the wheel has six spokes and a picture is taken every one sixth of a turn, the wheel will also appear stationary. If pictures are taken at a slightly faster rate, the wheel will not have made a complete turn between pictures; therefore, it will appear to be turning backwards.

24. Because of the Coriolis effect, the Gulf Stream, which flows northward out of the Caribbean, turns eastward. Its warm waters keep England and Western Europe at temperatures well above those in Newfoundland. (See page 120.)

25. To accelerate, the spaceship ejects gases from burned fuel at high speed. Because the ship pushes these gases, the gases push back on the ship causing it to move faster or to start moving if at rest. (See pages 75–83.)

26. The sharp edges of his skate blades enable the skater to cut into the ice so that he or she can push against the ice. To stop, the skater turns his blades so they scrape a thin layer of ice from the surface. The friction from this action slows the skater down. (See page 75.)

27. All small objects accelerate at about 32 feet per second per second when they fall. When a large object falls, it is its center of gravity that falls with an acceleration of 32 feet per second per second. The center of gravity of the smokestack is the point where the stack would balance if turned sideways. For the top of the smokestack to remain attached to the rest of the stack, it would have to move at a greater acceleration than the center of gravity. After all, it has a lot farther to fall. The materials holding the smokestack together are not strong enough to provide the force needed to make the top of the stack accelerate so much faster than the center of gravity. Consequently, the stack breaks apart after it has fallen partway. You can see this effect on a small scale, by building a tower of blocks and then pulling out the bottom block.

28. Both bullets will land at the same time. (See pages 88–90.)

29. Pulling is easier. It creates an upward as well as a for-

ward force. The upward force reduces the weight of the wheelbarrow pushing against the ground. The reduced weight means less friction, which makes the wheelbarrow easier to move.

30. The machine on the left won't work because there will never be enough balls moving downward to raise the ones that must be lifted. The machine on the right will stop because the water must be pumped to a point that is higher than the level from which it falls.

31. With a full roll, the applied force is farther from the center. This provides better leverage. (See page 123.)

32. (a), (b) Your fingers will meet at the center of the stick. (c) Your fingers will meet near the end that has the clay. The friction is greater where the weight is greater so your finger slides easier under the light side.

33. The photographer left his lens open for a few seconds as he rode along a busy highway. The lines of light were made by overhead lights, signs, and car and truck headlights. The camera rested on the dashboard. The lights in the lower part of the picture were reflected from the car's hood.

Index

Acceleration, 21–22, 65–69, 83, 158; defined, 74; *Graph* A, 22; zero, 69
Accelerometers, 65ff.; experiment, 65–66, 68, 69, *ill.* 65
Aerotrain, 6
Ai (three-toed sloth), 45
Air, *viii,* 19, 120
Air-blowing, experiment, 81–83
Air car, *viii,* 60–61
Airplanes, *vii, viii,* 1, 2, 19, 50; commercial jet liners, 14; experimental, *ill.* 12; gliders, 49; horsepower, 126; jets, 13, 79–80, 83, *ill.* 14; muscle-driven, 50; propeller, 13, 50; rocket, 13; speeds, 14, 19, 20, records, *viii,* 12–16; supersonic, 14. *See* Birds
Air resistance, 10, 14, 84
Air vehicles, 2
Albatross, 53
Aldrin, Edwin E., Jr., 110, *ill.* 111, 112, 113
Allen, Bryan, 50
American Museum of Natural History, The, 41, 51
American Power Boat Association, 5
Anemometer, 16, *ill.* 17
Animal locomotion, 36–54; birds, 48–54; fish, 36–40; horse, 40–44; muscle pairs, 46–48; special legs and feet, 44–45; speeds, 45–46
Animals: Burrowing, *viii;* cannon bone, 41, *ill.* 42; cat family, 46; hoppers, 44–45; jumpers, 44; legs (as pendulums), 96; long-distance runners, 45; primitive, 36; slowest, 45; speed records, *viii*
Antelope, 46, 48; pronghorn, 45
Ants, *viii*
Apollo 10, 16
Apollo 11, 110–11, 113
Armstrong, Neil A., 110, *ill.* 111, 112, 113
Astronauts, 55, 84, 110–13
Astronomers, 115
Atmosphere, 144
Atomic bomb, 139
Atomic energy, 122, 138–45
Atomic power plants, 140–41, *ill.* 140
Atomic reactors, 136
Atoms, 138ff.; E=mc², 139; fission, 139–41, 145; fusion, 141, 145
Auto races, 10; *Table* C, 10

Balloon rockets, *viii;* experiment, 81–83, *ill.* 82
Ball throwing, 34; measuring speed, *Table* J, 34–35
Bannister, Roger, 25
Barracuda, 37, *ill.* 37; speed, *Table* K, 39
Baseball: alternate paths, *ill.* 150; batted, 34; fast ball, 32–33, *ill.* 32; flight-path trajectories, 33
Bayi, Filbert, 27
Bedford, Dave, 27
Bell Aerospace, 12
Bell X-2 plane, 13
Bicycles, *viii, ix,* 85–86; centrifuge experiment, 74–75, *ill.* 75; Derby (1977), 12; gears, 28–32, 105, *ill.* 29; races, record, 31; ratios, *Table* H, 30; skids, 11–12; speedometer, 23; sprocket, 28, 30; ten-speed, 30; wheel experiments, 59, 105–6
Big mass, small mass experiment, 68–69
Big pull, little pull experiment, 67–68
Biology Teacher, The, 166
Birds, *vii,* 48–54; migration, 54; skeleton, 52, *ill.* 51; soaring, 52, 53
Blue Flame, 11
Boats: pitot tube, 19; speedometer, 19; speed records, 2–6, *Table* B, 4. *See also under* type boat
Bobsled, 27
Boeing 747 airliner, 126
Bonneville Salt Flats (Utah): speed records, 10–11, *ill.* 11
Boy Scout Bicycle Derby, 12
Brain Boosters, 166

Camel, 45
Camera, for measuring speed, 39
Campbell, Donald, 5–6
Campbell, Sir Malcolm, 5
Canal Electric Co., 135
Cape Kennedy, 111, 112
Caribbean, 121, 158
Cars, 1, 8, 68, 124; electric, 8; gasoline-powered, 8; "horseless carriage," 41; horsepower, 126; internal-combustion engine, 8; jet-powered, 11; piston-engined, 10–11; racing, 2, 10; "rocking," 96; seat belts, 61, 63; skids, 11;

Robert Gardner is head of the science department at Salisbury School, Salisbury, Connecticut, where he teaches physics, chemistry, and physical science. He has written several science books for children and numerous articles for *Nature and Science, The Science Teacher, The Biology Teacher, Science and Children, The Physics Teacher,* and *Current Science.* He is the author of another science experiment book for Doubleday, entitled *Magic Through Science.*

David Webster is a former elementary and junior high school science teacher and director of science for the Lincoln, Massachusetts, school system. For several years he wrote a regular feature for *Nature and Science.* He has written several puzzle books for Doubleday among which are *Brain Boosters, More Brain Boosters,* and *Crossroad Puzzlers.*

Both men were staff members of the Elementary Science Study of the Education Development Center and are coauthors of another Doubleday book, *Shadow Science.*